EYEWITNESS GUIDES

WATERCOLOUR

18th-century
Chinese fan

Gold leaf

Lapis
lazuli

13th-century
French bible
illustration

John Ruskin, *Study of a Velvet Crab*, c.1875

Medieval French
manuscript illumination

Watercolour
wallpaper design,
William Morris, 1875

12th-century Indian manuscript

EYEWITNESS 👁 GUIDES

WATERCOLOUR

MICHAEL CLARKE

Book illustrations
by William Blake

August Macke, *St. Germain, Near Tunis*, 1914

Miniature of
Sir Walter Raleigh

Silk fan design
by Camille
Pissarro, 1885

DORLING KINDERSLEY
LONDON • NEW YORK • SYDNEY

Watercolour box,
produced between
1766 and 1783

Franz Marc, *Two Blue Horses
in Front of a Red Rock*, 1913

Gum
arabic

Study
of mosaics
in the church of
Santa Costanza, Rome

DK

Dorling Kindersley
LONDON, NEW YORK, AUCKLAND, DELHI,
JOHANNESBURG, MUNICH, PARIS, and SYDNEY

For a full catalogue, visit
 www.dk.com

Editors Helen Castle and Ann Kay
Designer Claire Pegrum
Picture researcher Jo Evans
Editorial researcher Peter Jones
Assistant designer Simon Murrell
Senior editor Gwen Edmonds
Senior art editor Toni Kay
Managing editor Sean Moore
Managing art editor Tina Vaughan
DTP designer Doug Miller
DTP manager Joanna Figg-Latham
Production controller Meryl Silbert

This Eyewitness ® Guide
first published in Great Britain in 1993 by
Dorling Kindersley Limited,
9 Henrietta Street, London WC2E 8PS

2 4 6 8 10 9 7 5 3 1

Copyright © 1993 Dorling Kindersley Limited
Text copyright © 1993 Michael Clarke

A CIP catalogue record for this book is
available from the British Library

ISBN 0-7513-6152-6

Colour reproduction by Colourscan, Singapore
Printed in China by Toppan Printing Co.
(Shenzhen) Ltd.

The pigment-
producing
mineral,
cinnabar

Miniature of
Elizabeth I

Satirical Japanese painting,
late 19th century

Contents

Paul Cézanne, *The Three Bathers*, 1874–75

What is watercolour?

Cinnabar

Saffron

PIGMENTS
Pigments are either organic (vegetable, animal), like saffron, which is from a type of crocus, or inorganic (mineral), like cinnabar.

IN ITS BROADEST SENSE, WATERCOLOUR is any paint that is water-based – as opposed to being oil-based. The essential ingredients of watercolour are pigments (the substances that provide the colours), a binding agent (usually gum arabic), and water. When combined, these three components create transparent watercolour. However, if substances such as lead white (p. 62) are added, the watercolour becomes opaque. This opaque colour is called gouache or bodycolour (p. 62), and many of the paintings in this book are a mixture of transparent and opaque watercolour. Whatever the type of watercolour, the technique remains similar. Paint is thinned with water before being applied to a surface. Having spread the colour, the water evaporates, leaving pigment bound to the surface by the gum. When struck by light, the pigment gives off colour. Today, watercolours are usually painted on paper. Ancient civilizations such as the Egyptians, the Greeks, and the Romans, however, painted onto walls. In the Far East, silk was used, and medieval artists painted on parchment. Paper was invented in China and had become common in Europe by the 16th century. (*Unless otherwise stated, all watercolour works in this book are on paper.*)

CAVE PAINTING
Prehistoric watercolours, such as this one, which is about 20,000 years old, were made from berries or minerals (colour), saliva (binding), and water. This is from Pech-Merle, France.

THE PAINTINGS OF THE PHARAOHS
Many Egyptian watercolour paintings have survived since ancient times, protected in enclosed tombs. They were often applied straight onto the mud-plaster walls of the tombs. The above, however, was painted onto an upright wooden slab, in c.1250 B.C. On the right, it shows Deniu-en-Khons, a musician priestess, making an offering to the god Re-Harakhty. The paint is a type of tempera, made out of an opaque water-colour bound with gum or egg white.

Paint pot

Turquoise

Grinder

Lapis lazuli

Red ochre

Basalt palette

Twig paintbrush

Reed pens and palette

Twig paintbrush

Palette

ANCIENT EGYPTIAN TOOLS *left*
The sophisticated range of tools developed by the Egyptians helps to explain their painting methods. The grinder and palette (c.1250 B.C.) were used to prepare paint. Minerals – such as the red ochre, lapis lazuli, and turquoise shown here – would have been ground down to produce pigments. These pigments would then have been mixed with a binding agent and water on a palette, or in a paint pot, and applied to a surface with broad twig paintbrushes or finer reed pens.

CHINESE FAN *above*

The tradition of Chinese watercolour painting dates back over 2000 years, and is usually associated with the use of soft, transparent washes. However, gouache and precious metals were introduced in the 16th century, when a sophisticated tradition of portrait-painting started to develop. Watercolours were applied to a variety of surfaces, including silk, paper, and vellum. This fan, painted in 1727, is a combination of watercolour and ink on paper. Fan-painting became particularly popular in China in the 18th and 19th centuries. (*See p. 19 for more details about this fan.*)

A PERSIAN MANUSCRIPT *right*

This illustration to Shah Tahmasb's *Nizami Manuscript* shows the rich colour effects achieved by the use of gouache, an opaque watercolour, as opposed to simple transparent washes. The painting technique of Persian texts was intricate. It was also, in contrast to the use of washes, a gradual process of building up gouache and overlaying colours. The most precious of pigments, such as lapis lazuli, were even sorted grain by grain before application. (*See p. 18 for more details about this manuscript.*)

GUM ARABIC – THE BINDING AGENT

Gum arabic is taken from the sap of the acacia tree, and is the normal binding agent in watercolour. It ensures the even dispersal of paint, and an overall consistency of colour – by generally darkening tones. Gum arabic has a tendency to harden, so substances such as honey and glycerine are added to moisten it. Extra glycerine is needed in hot, dry countries. The 18th-century artist, Paul Sandby, working in Britain's cold climate, added gin to speed up the drying process.

TURNER – A MASTER OF THE WESTERN TRADITION

The pale washes of Turner's *View of the Campagna, Italy* (1819) contrast with the rich gouache of the Persian manuscript above. Although Turner used gouache in many of his paintings, he tended to emphasize the watery and spontaneous qualities of watercolour. He soaked the paper beforehand, so that the paint ran freely. He also created lighter areas by various methods, including rubbing the desired areas with wax. This wax repelled the watercolour, and was later removed to reveal white, unpainted paper. (*See p. 36 for more details about this painting.*)

Modern cake of watercolour

Cake paint applied to paper

19th-century cake-maker

The tubes of watercolour that are available today

MODERN MATERIALS

Watercolour cakes were first manufactured in the late 1700s, from pigment, gum arabic, and preservative. In 1846, Winsor and Newton started to produce watercolour in tubes – a moister form of paint.

The variety of watercolour

MAP OF GREAT BRITAIN
Matthew Paris; c.1250; ink and watercolour
Paris, a monk at the abbey of St. Albans near
London, was one of the main chroniclers
of 13th-century events. He often used
watercolour illustrations in his writings,
perhaps adding egg white to give adhesion.
In this early map of Britain, he used watercolour to pick out the sea and the rivers.

WATERCOLOUR HAS A LONG, VARIED HISTORY, which it owes to
its unique versatility. For centuries artists have exploited the fact
that the medium creates vivid colours, and is both fast-drying and
portable. Most of the works on these pages were never intended
to be "fine art". Early maps were often decorated with watercolour, and many architectural and garden plans were worked
out initially in watercolour, partly because drawn designs are
easily visible through watercolour washes. Before photography,
watercolour artists were vital members of foreign expeditions –
this convenient medium was ideal for recording exotic plants
and animals (p. 26). However,
it was not until the 19th
century that highly
finished water-
colours, such as
Cox's *Calais Pier*,
were produced
for exhibition.

THE MILITARY ROLL OF ARMS
English; before 1448; ink and bodycolour
These two jousting knights are from
a manuscript containing over 160
scenes. The strong colours possible with
bodycolour are well-suited to the bright
garments worn by medieval knights.

SAINT OTTILIE
*German (Swabian); c.1450; 26 x 18.5 cm
(10¼ x 7½ in); watercolour added to a woodcut print*
Woodcuts were the first printed images produced in the West. Simple watercolour washes
add interest to the strong lines of this print.

Study of a Mosaic Dome, Santa Costanza, Rome
PIETRO SANTI BARTOLI
c.1690–99; 42.5 x 31 cm (16¾ x 12¼ in); watercolour
Bartoli specialized in highly detailed engravings
of Roman antiquities. This watercolour study for an
engraving shows one half of a classical-style mosaic in the
dome of the church of Santa Costanza. Originally a tomb,
the building – and its mosaics – date from the fourth century.

WIMPOLE HALL, BEFORE AND AFTER "IMPROVEMENT"
Humphry Repton; 1801; 21 x 49.5 cm (8¼ x 19½ in); watercolour
The late 18th and early 19th centuries saw the era of English country house park design. Humphry Repton (1752–1818), a successful landscape gardener, was noted for showing accomplished watercolour designs to his clients. He presented these designs, along with notes, in book form – known as "Red Books" because they were bound in soft red leather. Special flaps (called "slides" by Repton) were a feature of his watercolour designs. The two photographs above are of the same watercolour – taken from Repton's Red Book on Wimpole Hall. In the left-hand photograph, the flap is down, giving a view of the front entrance of the hall before Repton's intended alterations. In the right-hand photograph, the flap has been lifted to reveal how Wimpole would look after the changes. Repton proposed to plant trees to mask the red stable buildings on the right, which he considered ugly.

CALAIS PIER *left*
David Cox; 1828; 16.5 x 27.5 cm (6½ x 10¾ in); watercolour
In Britain, the great age of watercolour was in the first half of the 19th century, and Cox (1783–1859) was one of the era's most successful artists. Watercolours of the scope and ambition of *Calais Pier* were intended to rival, if not surpass, oil paintings. Cox's technique here, with its broken touches of strong colouring, is almost Impressionist in effect. The dramatic subject of Calais Pier was a favourite with Cox, and he painted it on a number of occasions. In his *Treatise on Landscape Painting and Effect in Watercolours* (1841), he wrote: "Every tint should be laid on with clearness and decision ..."

Delicate washes of colour suggest fragile rose petals

ROSE (*ROSA DAMASCENA*) *right*
Pierre-Joseph Redouté; 1817; watercolour
Redouté was probably the greatest plant illustrator of his time, producing watercolours such as this one, and volumes of coloured prints. His subjects demanded astonishing precision and, during his career, he meticulously painted rare plants in the Royal Garden, Paris, and Kew Gardens, London.

DESIGN FOR DULWICH GALLERY *below*
Sir John Soane's architectural practice; 1811; 33 x 52 cm (13 x 20½ in); watercolour
By the late 18th century, making large numbers of architectural models had become costly, and architects were increasingly using watercolours to show clients some of the design stages. Soane did few watercolour illustrations himself; many were done by his assistant, J.M. Gandy. This gallery, in south London, was built in 1811–13.

One of a series of watercolour designs for the Dulwich Gallery

Illuminated texts

ILLUMINATED MANUSCRIPTS – hand-made books of text and pictures – were produced from later Roman times onwards, reaching a peak during the Middle Ages. The paints used were opaque, but they consisted of ground pigments mixed with a binding agent and diluted with water – making these manuscripts the ancestors of modern-day watercolours. "Glair" (egg white) was the usual binding agent, although by the 14th century, gum arabic was more popular. Illuminated texts were written and painted on vellum or parchment (animal skin) and many medieval manuscripts were decorated with gold. Most of the texts were religious, although subjects such as the story of King Arthur, medical treatises, and Greek and Roman classics, were also illustrated.

AN ARTIST AT WORK
This detail is from *A King and Queen* (p. 11). Most early medieval texts were produced by monks, and the text and pictures were usually executed by the same person.

JACOB WRESTLING WITH THE ANGELS
Vienna Genesis Bible; c.700; 21 x 13 cm (8¼ x 5 in)
This image contains several scenes, all linked together pictorially. Like many opulent early manuscripts, it is painted on stained purple vellum – purple dye was extremely costly.

BEGINNING OF ST. JOHN'S GOSPEL
Arnstein Bible; 1175; 54.5 x 36 cm (21½ x 14½ in)
The opening words of the Proverbs and the Gospels were often illuminated. Here, St. John forms part of the initial letter. Later manuscripts such as this were more harmonious in colour than early Christian texts.

St. John

LINDISFARNE GOSPEL *698; 34 x 25 cm (13 x 10 in)*
The spread of Christianity increased the need amongst missionaries for religious texts. This famous example was made on Lindisfarne ("holy island"), off the north-east coast of England. The yellowed animal skin on which it is painted is clearly visible.

Imago aequilae

THE CRUCIFIXION
French Psalter; c.1215;
17 x 12 cm (6¾ x 4¾ in)
Brightly coloured, with a substantial amount of expensive gold leaf, this illustration is from a Psalter, or Book of Psalms. Its rare and precious appearance is entirely intentional. In using expensive materials, the various patrons of illuminated manuscripts not only honoured the holy texts, but also made a lavish display of their own devotion.

Vellum has an extremely fine grain

VELLUM
Many illuminations were painted onto vellum, a particularly fine parchment prepared from the skin of young animals.

A KING AND QUEEN AND A CLERIC INSTRUCTING AN ARTIST
French Moralized Bible; c.1220
This miniature is a fascinating depiction of patronage in the Middle Ages. A king and queen are shown above a cleric, who is instructing an artist how to write and paint. It was quite common for a patron's portrait to be included in a text.

SIEGE WARFARE
Flemish Book of Hours; c.1300; 9.5 x 7 cm (3¾ x 2¾ in)
This is a marginal illustration from a tiny Book of Hours – a collection of religious texts intended for private use. Pictures were often placed in margins, as these were the less important parts of the manuscripts. Images were often deliberately amusing. Here, animals act the roles of men.

THE BAPTISM OF CONSTANTINE
Giovanni dei Corradi; 1451; 56 x 43 cm (22 x 17 in)
This scene is set in the initial "P" of the text. "Historiated" (containing a story) initials were common in illuminated manuscripts. Here, the text is set to music. The careful ruling of lines, so important in manuscript illumination, is also evident.

The Limbourgs

PAUL LIMBOURG
The eldest brother's portrait appears on the January calendar page of the *Très Riches Heures* (below left).

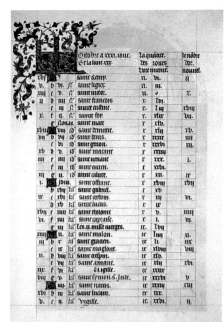

WIDELY ACKNOWLEDGED to be the greatest manuscript illuminators, the Limbourg brothers – Jean, Herman, and Paul – came from Nijmegen in what is now Holland. The brothers (all of whom, it seems, had died by 1416) were employed in the early 15th century by one of the most remarkable art patrons of the late Middle Ages – the French landowner, Jean, Duke of Berry. For him, they painted some of the most beautiful and lavish of all illuminated manuscripts, such as the *Belles Heures* ("Beautiful Book of Hours") and the *Très Riches Heures* ("Very Rich Book of Hours"). Their work is possibly the most sophisticated predecessor of modern watercolour painting. To achieve the extraordinarily precise detail, the Limbourgs chose extremely fine brushes, and probably used magnifying lenses.

CALENDAR
The *Très Riches Heures* begins with a spectacular series of whole-page illustrations of the months of the year. Before each month is a page with that month's calendar written out. This is the calendar for January. The scribe's ruling lines are visible and the page is decorated with richly coloured foliate patterns. The coloured pigments were mixed with water and gum – as well as binding the pigment and making colour adhere to the vellum, gum acted as an effective preservative.

The Très Riches Heures

THE LIMBOURG BROTHERS *1413–16 (left unfinished; completed by Jean Colombe c.1485); 206 bound sheets of fine vellum; each page: 29 x 21 cm (11½ x 8¼ in)*

Medieval "Books of Hours" contained Bible extracts and prayers for each hour of the day, and often included calendars. The paintings shown here all come from the *Très Riches Heures,* and represent the summit of the illuminator's art.

JANUARY *left*
Here, the Duke of Berry, wearing a hat, is seated at table. The occasion shown is the day when seasonal gifts were traditionally exchanged and guests invited to table. The vivid pigments used were obtained from minerals, plants, or chemicals.

FEBRUARY *right*
This month, frequently the hardest and bleakest of the year, has been captured with a vividly detailed realism. From the all-white landscape and the weak wintry light, to the leaden grey sky and the hungry birds pecking at the corn, nothing has escaped the artist's highly original observation. An amusingly coarse note is struck by the foreground figures, seen exposing their bodies to the warmth of the fire.

MARCH
Here, in the landscape overlooked by the Duke of Berry's château at Lusignan, the year's agricultural work begins. The brothers were masters of atmospheric perspective, whereby, as in this scene, forms tend to soften and lighten near the horizon.

OCTOBER

The Duke's Parisian residence, the Hôtel de Nesle, is shown in the background of this scene of ploughing and sowing. The Limbourgs' landscapes were highly naturalistic, and the Hôtel building is so precisely depicted that a model of it has been made, based on the details shown here.

GOLDS AND BLUES

The brothers fully exploited the richness of gold, either added to pigments and painted on, or as gold leaf, often glazed with green or red. Their skies, a deep, luminous, yet transparent blue, were painted in ultramarine, which was made from costly oriental lapis lazuli.

Gold leaf

Lapis lazuli

THE GARDEN OF EDEN

The Garden of Eden was placed a little farther along in the *Très Riches Heures*, after the illustrations to the months. It shows the story, told in the Book of Genesis, of the Temptation and Expulsion of Adam and Eve from the Garden of Eden. The figure type of Eve, with her swelling belly and graceful outlines, conforms to what was fashionable in northern Europe at the time. As in all their miniatures, the Limbourgs have made extensive use of gold leaf, even more so here than usual. Their placing of an essentially circular composition in the centre of a rectangular page is particularly daring.

THE TEMPTATION

Eve takes the apple from the serpent, and tempts Adam. Adam and Eve's pale bodies stand out vividly against the strong green of the background.

The architecture has a highly convincing three-dimensional realism

THE EXPULSION

Adam and Eve pass through the gates of the Garden of Eden, banished from Paradise forever.

A transparent quality has been given to the water

Nature into art

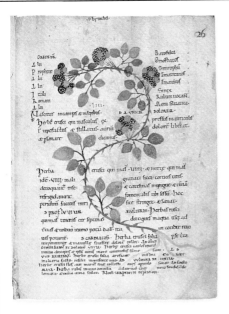

FOR CENTURIES, WATERCOLOUR was the medium chosen for making accurate plant and animal studies, and so played a part in helping to advance scientific learning. Watercolour had been used since medieval times to illustrate "herbals" – books that described the properties of medicinal herbs. From the 15th century onwards, expeditions to the Americas and the Far East brought many new animal and plant species back to Europe (pp. 26–27). These were often recorded in watercolour, which was both quick to apply and fast-drying (specimens might decompose), and allowed a high degree of detailed accuracy.

A BRAMBLE (*RUBUS FRUTICOSUS*)
English; c.1120; 26 x 20 cm (10¼ x 7¾ in);
pen and watercolour on vellum
This manuscript was produced in Bury St. Edmunds, Suffolk. The bramble illustrates a text – originally written about A.D. 400 – which describes herbal remedies derived from plants. During the Middle Ages, this type of knowledge was preserved in religious institutions such as monasteries, and this illustration was almost certainly produced by a monk.

DETAILED DEPICTION
Painted studies of plants and animals had to achieve the degree of detail later captured by photographs – such as this picture of a bramble.

Painting the natural world

Nature studies were all basically stimulated by people's desire to know as much as possible about the world they inhabited. It was watercolour painters who often provided the first accurate images of plants and animals from newly explored lands (pp. 26–27). The illustrations on these pages show a progression from essentially factual drawings to studies that were very much works of art in their own right.

A.M. 3267.ª '56.   V. A. M.

A PARROT, BUTTERFLIES, MOTH, AND MUSCADINE GRAPES
Samuel Dixon; c.1755; 30.5 x 40.5 cm (12 x 16 in); watercolour and bodycolour
Dixon's nature pieces – painted in relatively thick colour, on embossed paper – had a life-like, almost three-dimensional appearance. They were highly popular in his native Dublin.

DAFFODILS AND RED ADMIRAL BUTTERFLY
Jacques Le Moyne de Morgues; c.1586; 27.5 x 19 cm (11 x 7½ in); watercolour and bodycolour
Le Moyne painted flowers and fruits seen in 16th-century English gardens. He usually applied thin watercolour washes over drawings, adding very little bodycolour.

STUDY OF A VELVET CRAB
John Ruskin; c.1875; 24.5 x 31.5 cm
(9¾ x 12½ in); watercolour and bodycolour over pencil
The most influential English art critic of the 19th century, John Ruskin
(1819–1900) championed Turner (pp. 36–37), the Pre-Raphaelites (pp. 46–47),
and watercolour painting in general. A talented watercolourist himself, the
precision of this piece recalls Dürer's nature studies (pp. 16–17). Ruskin, a
professor of art at Oxford, probably used it as a teaching aid.

JUMPING TROUT
Winslow Homer; 1889; 31.5 x 49.5 cm
(12½ x 19½ in); watercolour and pencil
Homer (1836–1910) was one of the
greatest American watercolourists.
He fully exploited the qualities of
watercolour to express his love of
the sea and marine subjects. In this
superb drawing, he seems, almost
photographically, to have caught
the moment when the fish leaps
dramatically from the water.

HOMER'S WATERCOLOUR BOX
These watercolour paints, in a
portable canvas pouch, were
used by Winslow Homer.
Homer obviously relished the
spontaneity of the medium – he
planned many of his fishing
trips so that he could combine
his twin passions of sketching
and angling. Detailed realism
was important: "I paint it [the
subject] exactly as it appears."

Watercolour's first master

ALBRECHT DÜRER (1471–1528) is often regarded as the first all-round master of watercolour. Almost half of his existing output was painted in the medium, and his technique was sophisticated for the time – he used pen and ink for outlines, opaque colours to show volume, and clear washes for light effects. Dürer would have seen many illuminated texts and coloured woodcuts, but it was not until he started travelling that he filled his sketchbooks with washed drawings. In these, he was unrestrained by patrons' demands, and so chose to focus on landscapes and nature studies. In many ways, his enquiring approach to landscape anticipated the best of the great 19th-century watercolour tradition.

THREE STUDIES OF A HELMET
Albrecht Dürer; c.1500; original paper size:
42 x 27 cm (16½ x 10½ in); pen and watercolour
These tournament jousting helmets show the way in which Dürer mixed media. For instance, in the helmet on the right, he chose to sketch first in pen, before transferring to brushwork alone.

A HOUSE ON AN ISLAND IN A POND
Albrecht Dürer; 1496–97; 21.5 x 22 cm
(8¼ x 8¾ in); watercolour and bodycolour
Dürer "discovered" the landscape watercolour, combining transparent and opaque colours to great atmospheric effect. This fisherman's house stood on the outskirts of Nuremberg, in Germany.

SELF-PORTRAIT
Albrecht Dürer; 1500; 170 x
124.5 cm (67 x 49 in); oil on canvas
"Thus, I, Albrecht Dürer, from Nuremberg, painted myself with indelible colours at the age of 28." Dürer was by this time already a learned man. Having received a classical education, he was apprenticed to a painter, and then travelled widely. When in northern Italy, he was profoundly influenced by the art of the Italian masters.

STAG BEETLE
Albrecht Dürer; 1505; 14 x 11.5 cm
(5½ x 4½ in); watercolour and bodycolour
Dürer's many detailed watercolours of plants and animals effectively began the tradition of using watercolour for scientific drawings (pp. 14–15).

DÜRER'S DREAM (LANDSCAPE FLOODED WITH WATERS FROM HEAVEN)
Albrecht Dürer; 1525; 30 x 42 cm
(11¾ x 16½ in); pen and watercolour
"In the night between Wednesday and Thursday after Whitsunday [30–31 May] I saw this appearance in my sleep ..." Dürer's watercolour sketch and handwritten text describe a cataclysmic rainstorm, which preceded a disastrous flood that had been widely prophesied in 1525.

Val d'Arco: View of a Small Town with a Fortified Castle

ALBRECHT DÜRER *1495; 22.5 x 22.5 cm*
(8¾ x 8¾ in); watercolour and bodycolour

This is one of Dürer's greatest landscape paintings. Its eerie luminosity was obtained by the use of various greens, laid one over the other, and by the blue-greys that distinguish the rock faces. He probably painted this when returning from his first visit to Italy. Although travel was inspiring for Dürer, it was also a necessity – in this period plague raged through his native Nuremberg.

DETAIL OF A HILL TOWN
The acute powers of observation that Dürer often employed in his watercolours are well illustrated by this detail of a fortified hill town, set high up on a dramatic mountain crag. It is quite possible that Dürer himself would have stopped here for refreshment, or even a brief stay, on his homeward journey.

Eastern approaches

WATER-SOLUBLE PAINTS have been used throughout the Eastern world for many centuries – from the east coast of Africa, and the Middle East, to Japan. Equivalents of the modern watercolour were known in China during the first century B.C. About 2000 years ago, Chinese artists began to paint watercolours onto screens and scrolls made of silk. It was the Chinese who invented the first paper, in A.D. 105, and Far Eastern artists who then perfected a technique of painting on both silk and paper with watercolours and ink. A strong landscape tradition developed in China, while the Japanese tended to choose more intimate subject-matter, for example in their 18th- and 19th-century drawings of actors and courtesans. In Persia (now Iran), the simple drawing and transparent washes of the 10th and 11th centuries were gradually replaced by richly decorated manuscripts, with intense, layered colouring.

ANIMALS AND THEIR USES *above Arabic; 13th century; 24 x 15 cm (9½ x 6 in); gouache and ink*
By the 13th century, Islamic workmanship had reached a high level of expertise. This illustration of a hare is from a work on the medicinal properties of parts of animals.

SHAH TAHMASB'S NIZAMI MANUSCRIPT
Persian; c.1540; 36 x 25 cm (14 x 10 in); ink, gouache, and gold leaf
Shah Tahmasb commissioned this edition of the poems of Nizami, which was painted by various court artists. The strong outlines of the figures were first painted in with a reed pen or a fine brush. Opaque colours were then progressively overlaid, using glues or gum arabic for binding, and brushes made from squirrel or kitten hairs, set in birds'-feather quills.

Nightmare of Demons & Chimeras
KYOSAI *(Japanese) c.1885; 17 x 6 cm (7 x 2 in); ink and watercolour*
Kyosai's satirical work, which is almost cartoon-like, appears to have been painted at great speed. Kyosai would lay on a wash with one brush, whilst "diluting" the colour on the paper with a second brush filled with water.

THE ANCIENT PINE OF DONG MON

*Gao Fengham (Chinese); 1727; maximum width:
53 cm (21 in); ink and watercolour on paper fan*

The painter belonged to a group known as the
Eccentric Masters of Yangzhou. He recalled
how pine trees in a certain area reminded
him of dragons: "I used to choose the
pines of Huangshan to paint the
unusual crouching dragons
stretching out in strange and
different shapes." Apart
from the main inscription
across the top, there
is a further poem on
the left of the fan.

The delicately observed tree
displays the traditional
Chinese interest in
natural forms

*The tree is
shaped like
a dragon*

FANS IN THE WEST

The fan was a form that was
particularly associated with the
East – although it was also used
on occasion by the Impressionists.

TWO POPULAR ETHIOPIAN SAINTS

*Gondar (Ethiopian); 18th century; 28 x 21.5 cm
(11 x 8½ in); gouache and ink on vellum*

This illustration was painted with thick,
simple colours derived from vegetable
pigments. With the influence of Italian
and Portuguese missionaries in the 16th
and 17th centuries, Ethiopians began
to produce illustrated texts depicting
Christian saints from Africa. Two
African saints – Tokla Haymanot and
Gabra Manfas Qeddus – are seen here.

PORTRAIT OF CAI SHIYING

*Chinese; 17th century; 139 x 99 cm
(76 x 39 in); ink, gouache, and watercolour*

Chinese portraits of this period indicated
the sitter's importance and power. In this
case, the highest quality pigments were
used: ultramarine and azurite for blue;
malachite and verdigris for green.

THE ADVENTURES OF PRINCE PANJI

*Indonesian; c.1805;
illustration: 12.5 x 16 cm
(5 x 6¼ in); ink and gouache*

This illustrates a Javanese
tale that goes back to the
15th century. It chronicles
the amorous adventures
of Prince Panji, prince of
Koripan. The use of bright
gouache on highly stylized
figures is typically Eastern.
Western influences are
evident, however, in the
Dutch flags of the ships.

A BRILLIANT BLUE SEA

The way in which gouache
has been overlaid gives the
sea real depth. A brilliant
blue shines through a darker
colour applied over the top.

The art of India

THE INDIAN SUB-CONTINENT has a long tradition of producing manuscript illuminations. These were executed in gouache, at first on palm leaves and then later, with the Muslim invasion in the 13th century, on paper. Early examples were inspired by the Hindu and Jain religions, and earthy colours were used. The Mogul Dynasty, which governed from the 16th to 18th centuries, transformed this tradition into one of courtly art; richly-coloured illustrations were created through a repeated layering of gouache, followed by burnishing (rubbing away at the paint surface). By the 19th century, the patronage of Europeans led to the choice of more subdued subjects – frequently natural history paintings and portraits – and the use of lighter washes and less vibrant colouring.

The Bodhisattva Manjusri

c.1145; central image: 7 x 7 cm (2¾ x 2¾ in); bodycolour on palm leaf
Painted on palm leaf, this pre-dates the introduction of paper. It is taken from *The Perfection of Wisdom*, and features one of the main Bodhisattva – Buddhist gods who choose to remain on earth as spiritual guides.

A MONK RESISTING THE ATTRACTIONS OF WOMEN
1460; 11.5 x 29.5 cm (4½ x 11½ in); ink and gouache
This manuscript describes the teachings of the founder of Jainism, and sets out rules of behaviour for monks. Crimson and ultramarine pigments are used lavishly.

AKBAR'S TRIUMPHANT ENTRY INTO SURAT
c.1590; 32 x 19 cm (12½ x 7½ in); gouache
This illustration is from the history of the Mogul Dynasty, the *Akbarnama*, which was presented to the Emperor Akbar in 1590. It was painted on a thick rag-based paper that was prepared by burnishing, and then painted with layer upon layer of pigment built up to a rich colouring. It would have taken a number of artists to complete such a manuscript, since it took two artists to produce each picture. The senior one provided the outline design and details such as faces, while the junior one did all the preparation and colouring.

THE AWAKENING OF KUMBHAKARNA
Sahib Din; 1652; 21 x 35 cm (8¼ x 13¾ in); gouache
Din's illustration is from the epic, *Ramayana*, a mythical tale that was based on historical fact. It shows the sleeping giant Kumbhakarna, who is woken up in order to defend his brother Ravana from the attack of Rama and his monkey allies.

Even minor characters have been lent drama and interest by the artist

THE TOILS OF LOVE
c.1590–1600; 17 x 9 cm (6½ x 3½ in); gouache
This is in the rich Bijapuri style of painting. Bijapur was one of the three sultanates of the Deccan (central southern India), and remained independent of Mogul rule until 1686–87. The story is a romance composed in 1591 by Hasan Manjhu Khalij. Here, the hero and heroine, Shahji and Mahji, conduct an interview through a curtain.

The stylized gesture of this figure is a good illustration of the static courtly style of the period

THE BOOK OF CREATION *below*
1836; 24 x 64.5 cm (9½ x 25¼ in); gouache on aloe bark
Filled with flora and fauna, this opulent manuscript represents a last great outburst of Assamese (northern Indian) art. It demonstrates how, in parts of India, the old traditional techniques and forms persisted for centuries after the introduction of the realistic styles of the Mogul artists.
The Book of Creation is a Hindu religious text that was popular at the time.

Here, Krishna (a Hindu god) is shown dancing with milkmaids in the circle of love

HAWK OR PEREGRINE
1802; 46.5 x 27.5 cm (18¼ x 10¾ in); watercolour
This was presented to the British Resident in India by a Raja (Indian prince). It is painted in "European-style" transparent washes, rather than the traditional opaque colour.

Miniature painting

Red pigment

SHADES OF RED
Red was used as the ground for many miniatures. The pigments used came from a variety of animal and vegetable sources.

THE ART OF THE MINIATURE painter or "limner" developed in the 16th century, and was descended from that of the illuminator of medieval manuscripts (pp. 10–13). Miniatures were small portraits, frequently requiring painstakingly detailed work by the artist. They were either carried around, worn as lockets, or sent as tokens – for example to a prospective marriage partner. Early examples were painted in watercolour on discs of fine parchment, which were stuck onto card. Gouache was also used and, in the 18th century, parchment was replaced by ivory as the normal painting surface. Ivory is even smoother and less absorbent than parchment. This allowed artists either to apply a thin, transparent colour wash and let the luminous ivory shine through – for example on facial features – or build up thick colour. In the 19th century, quite large miniatures, the size of small paintings, were produced on thin sheets of rolled out ivory.

HOLBEIN'S MINIATURES
Holbein used mainly grey and red transparent watercolours, over a base colour of carnation – rose-pink.

MRS PEMBERTON
Hans Holbein; c.1536; 5 cm (2 in) across; watercolour and bodycolour on vellum
Holbein, a German artist who was Henry VIII's painter, brought a new realism to miniatures.

HANS HOLBEIN
Lucas Hornebolte; c.1547; 4.5 cm (1¾ in); watercolour and bodycolour on vellum
It was Hornebolte who taught Holbein how to use watercolour and bodycolour on vellum.

SIR THOMAS MORE
More, who was later made a saint, sits to the right of his father, Sir John More, who is shown wearing red judge's robes.

LOCKEY'S INSPIRATION
Lockey (c.1565–1616) copied this composition from a drawing of the same subject, now lost, by Holbein. He has, however, changed the background on the right.

The Family of Sir Thomas More
ROWLAND LOCKEY
c.1593; 24 x 29 cm (9½ x 11½ in); watercolour and bodycolour on vellum

The style of this unusually large miniature is very like that of Hilliard (pp. 24–25). A contemporary called Lockey "[Hilliard's] expert scholler ... skilful in limning." More – Henry VIII's Lord Chancellor – lost his life for refusing to approve the King's divorce from Queen Catherine.

Baroness Burdett-Coutts
SIR WILLIAM CHARLES ROSS
c.1847; 42 x 29 cm (16½ x 11½ in);
watercolour and gouache on ivory

This large, elegant portrait shows how, by this date, miniatures were trying to rival oil paintings for grandeur of effect. For example, square miniatures were replacing oval ones – in 1803, one miniaturist dismissed oval miniatures as "toys". Ross (c.1794–1860) mixed a lot of gum with his colours, giving them a rich sheen, but used little gouache, saving it for the brightest areas of his paintings.

SIR THOMAS STEPNEY
George Engleheart; c.1775–80; 5 x 4 cm
(2 x 1½ in); watercolour and gouache on ivory
Engleheart allows the polished surface of the ivory to shine through, and mainly transparent watercolour is used. He has painted vertical strokes of blue-grey or pink onto a pale, flesh-coloured wash, adding gouache for the clothing and background.

1811 miniature of William Reeves, a nephew of the founder of Reeves

A MINIATURIST AT WORK
This pen and pencil drawing (c.1815–20) by Mary Grimaldi shows her father-in-law William Grimaldi – miniaturist to George III and George IV. The angled stand on the desk enabled the miniature to be raised up so that the artist could work without excessive strain.

PORTABLE MINIATURIST'S EASEL
This type of easel was used in the 18th and 19th centuries. The drawer stored equipment such as brushes (squirrel or sable), a water bowl, ivory palettes, and pots of paint (or commercially made cakes of paint after about 1800).

Portrait of an era

THE WORK OF NICHOLAS HILLIARD (1547–1619), the first great British miniaturist (pp. 22–23), provides a vivid picture of Elizabethan and Jacobean life. Elizabeth I's miniaturist, he applied flesh tints with delicate washes, drawing in facial features with a pen, as he explained: "… little light touches with colour very thin, and like hatches, as we call it, with the pen." Hilliard considered Holbein (p. 22) to be "the greatest master", and was also influenced by "the most excellent Albrecht Dürer" (pp. 16–17). His early portraits were circular, but he soon adopted the oval format, which gave more scope for depicting the elaborate costume of the day. By the 1580s, he was producing large, rectangular portraits with intricate backgrounds. In his treatise on miniature painting, Hilliard claimed that the art "tendeth not to common men's use", and that artists should "take heed of the dandruff of the head shedding from the hair."

SELF-PORTRAIT
Nicholas Hilliard; 1577; 4 cm (1½ in) across; watercolour and bodycolour on vellum
Hilliard depicts himself aged 30, the year after he had married. This miniature forms a companion to one of the artist's father.

Front cover

Ruby

Diamond

THE HENEAGE ("ARMADA") JEWEL
Nicholas Hilliard; whole pendant: c.1588; miniature inside: 1580; 7 x 5 cm (2¾ x 2 in); watercolour and bodycolour on vellum
This pendant opens to reveal a portrait of Elizabeth, who gave it to Sir Thomas Heneage on the defeat of the Spanish Armada. The jewelled frame is enamel and gold. Elizabeth disliked the use of shadow – like many Hilliard portraits, this one is rather two-dimensional.

GEORGE CLIFFORD, THIRD EARL OF CUMBERLAND, AS THE KNIGHT OF PENDRAGON CASTLE *left*
Nicholas Hilliard; c.1590; 25.5 x 18 cm (10 x 7 in); watercolour and bodycolour on vellum
Despite the freely painted background, this is a highly finished work. Apparently monumental in scale, the magnificent, full-length portrait is in fact quite small (although it is Hilliard's largest surviving miniature). Clifford, a buccaneer and courtier, enjoyed Elizabeth I's favour – he wears her diamond-set glove in his hat.

SIR WALTER RALEIGH
Nicholas Hilliard; c.1585; 5 x 4.5 cm (2 x 1¾ in); watercolour and bodycolour on vellum
Here, the adventurer is depicted very much as a courtier. Hilliard used Dürer's rule "that the forehead is of the length of the nose, and the nose as long as from the nose to the chin."

Hilliard used a mussel shell,
such as this, as his palette.
He bought his pigments
at an apothecary's shop
(the equivalent of the
present-day chemist),
and ground them up.
In the shell, he would
have mixed the pigment
with a binding agent, such
as gum arabic. If the paint
was still too dry, some "sugar
candy" was added, and if the
colour did not take well, because
a "sweaty hand or fatty finger
hath touched your parchment",
then a little earwax was added!

Mussel
shell

Young Man Among Roses
NICHOLAS HILLIARD
c.1587; 13.5 x 7.5 cm (5¼ x 2¾ in);
watercolour and bodycolour on vellum

This famous image probably shows
Robert Devereux, second earl of
Essex. He is clothed in Elizabeth
I's colours, black and white, and
surrounded by eglantine (a wild
rose), one of her favourite flowers.
The inscription at the top translates
as: "My praised faith causes my
sufferings." Essex may have been
trying to appease the Queen, who
was reportedly displeased at his
marriage to the widow of another
favourite, Sir Philip Sidney. The
colours used reflect Hilliard's belief
that: "besides black and white, there
are but five other principal colours ...
murrey [deep red or purple], red,
blue, green, and yellow."

FINE DETAIL
The realistically
painted plants –
compare the detail
above with the photograph on the
right – are shown with the same accuracy
as the plant decoration of medieval texts.
Their meaning is linked to the symbolism
associated with roses: joy and pain, love
and purity. The pricks of the thorns could
be compared to the wounds of love.

The wild
rose eglantine
(or "sweet brier")

Exploring new worlds

WATERCOLOURS PAINTED by early travellers were vital to the documentation of new worlds. The age of exploration began in Europe with the Renaissance, with men like Christopher Columbus. Soon, there was a demand for accurate reporting of what had been seen. In the late 16th century, explorers began to use drawings to illustrate verbal and written reports, and watercolour was frequently used to add colour. By the 18th century, as commercial links were forged between Europe and the rest of the world, embassies and scientific expeditions often employed specialist watercolourists such as William Alexander. By this time, watercolour was gaining in stature, and many sketches were worked up into finished paintings for public exhibition.

MAPPING THE WORLD
This is a map of the empires and the countries of the world in 1846. It shows how, by the mid-19th century, European nations had claimed most of the previously "undiscovered" parts of the world as their own. England, for instance, is coloured pink, along with its colonies, such as Canada and Australia.

Livingstone's compass

OPENING UP AFRICA
This compass belonged to Scottish missionary Dr. David Livingstone, who explored vast areas of Africa between the 1840s and 1870s.

Eskimo Woman and Baby
JOHN WHITE *c.1585–90;*
22 x 16.5 cm (8¾ x 6½ in); pencil, watercolour, and bodycolour
White (1575–93), the earliest European watercolourist to paint American scenes, sailed with the fleet that established the first English colony in North America. His style was simple – limited colours, with white bodycolour for highlights – as his principal aim was to record what he saw.

The towne of Pomeiooh and true forme of their howses, covered and enclosed some wth matts, and some wth barcks of trees. All compassed about wth smale poles stock thick together in steed of a wall.

THE VILLAGE OF POMEIOOC
John White; c.1585–93; 22 x 21.5 cm (8¾ x 8½ in); pencil, watercolour, and gold bodycolour
This study of a fortified Indian village has been outlined first with a lead pencil. Watercolour was then applied directly onto untreated paper. The preparatory sketch was later touched up with black watercolour.

Part of the Castle of Tangier

A PROSPECT OF THE LAND AND FORTS … BEFORE TANGIER DRAWNE FROM PETERBOROW TOWER
Wenceslaus Hollar; 1669; 28 x 102 cm (11 x 40¼ in);
pen and ink with watercolour on nine joined pieces of paper
Hollar accompanied an expedition to Tangier, in North Africa, in 1669. "Designer of prospects" to Charles II, his task was to draw and map the area, recently acquired by the English king. Czech-born Hollar was primarily a printmaker – evident from his simple technique. This watercolour uses a deliberately limited range of blues and greens to produce a functional record of the Tangier walls.

CHINESE BARGES OF LORD MACARTNEY'S EMBASSY, PREPARING TO PASS UNDER A BRIDGE
William Alexander; 1796; 30.5 x 46 cm (12 x 18 in); watercolour
Alexander accompanied a British trip to China in 1793–94. Once back in England, he painted watercolours based on his on-the-spot sketches; the absence of pencil drawing suggests that this is one of these later works, rather than a sketch.

COLUMNS OF THE TEMPLE ZEUS, AT ATHENS
Dominique Papety; 1846; 41.5 x 29 cm (16¼ x 11½ in); pencil and watercolour
In 1847, the French artist Papety published an account of his travels in Greece. His work was influential in France, turning the attention of artists such as Ingres (p. 54) to ancient Grecian, rather than Roman, art. Here, he uses watercolour over a black lead sketch.

THE THEATRE AT MILETUS
William Pars; c.1765; 29.5 x 47 cm (11½ x 18½ in); pen, watercolour, gum arabic
Pars joined an expedition exploring the antiquities of Asia Minor in 1764. His use of pen is highly effective – here, it seems to have been dipped in grey wash; ink is reserved for dark areas and the foreground. With its pale washes, the temple takes second place to the foreground group, shown in intense colour and strong ink-work.

COLLECTING SAMPLES
This leather satchel (left) was used by the English explorer and botanist Sir Joseph Hooker throughout his travels. He placed any interesting plant species that he came across into this bag. Having collected such samples, it was vital that they be recorded by artists, who became key members of the great 19th-century expeditions. Hooker travelled widely during the mid- and late 19th century. He accompanied Sir James Ross's 1839 expedition to the Arctic, and explored many parts of Asia.

19th-century botanist's satchel

The portable art

FOR 18TH- AND 19TH-CENTURY travellers and tourists, sketching in watercolour was the perfect way to record their tours. It was particularly suitable because the light, minimal materials were easy to carry. Spurred on by a mix of natural curiosity, fashion, and newly published guide-books, people journeyed surprising distances. Italy, with its classical sites, was one of the most popular destinations. A visit to Rome became, at this time, a compulsory part of the "Grand Tour" – the long European journey that it was fashionable for young aristocrats to make. More distant countries, such as Egypt, came into reach by the mid-19th century, when the equivalent of a "package tour" could be arranged.

AN ARTIST TRAVELLING IN WALES
Thomas Rowlandson; 1799;
26.5 x 32.5 cm (10½ x 12¾ in); aquatint print
This tongue-in-cheek print makes fun of the travelling artist, prepared to cross the Welsh countryside even in atrocious weather. Expense was also an obstacle to painters making sketching trips. On a tour of North Wales, in 1835, Samuel Palmer (p. 42) wrote, "Had I conceived how much it would cost I would as soon have started for the United States as Wales."

PORTABLE PAINT BOX
T. Reeves & Son, the makers of artists' materials, produced this wooden watercolour box from 1766 to 1783. The inclusion of a tray for mixing paints and a built-in water pot meant that it was not only portable, but also suitable for painting out of doors on location.

RUINS OF PAESTUM, NEAR SALERNO: THE THREE TEMPLES
John Robert Cozens; 1782;
26 x 36 cm (10 x 14½ in); watercolour
Cozens (1752–97) was the artist who opened British eyes to the beauty of the Italian landscape. He made several trips to Italy, employed as a travelling artist to record the sights. In 1782–83, he accompanied his rich patron William Hamilton there, filling seven sketchbooks with drawings. These he used later as the basis for the fully worked-up Italian watercolours that he produced for British clients. This view is of the ancient Greek temples at Paestum, in southern Italy.

MESSIEURS LES VOYAGEURS IN A SNOW DRIFT UPON MOUNT TARRAR
J.M.W. Turner; 1829; 54.5 x 75 cm
(21½ x 29½ in); watercolour and bodycolour
For the subjects of his paintings, Turner (1775–1851) was dependent on the sketching tours that he undertook once or twice a year. In Italy, he was particularly inspired by the strength of the light that he encountered there, which was so different to that of his native England. This watercolour records Turner's hazardous journey home from his second trip to Italy, in 1828–29. All travellers had to pass over the Alps by "diligence" (stagecoach). He recalled, "the snow began to fall at Foligno, tho' more of ice than snow, so that the coach from its weight slide about in all directions ... till at Sarre-valli the diligence slid into a ditch, and required six oxen, sent three miles back for, to drag it out ..."

Tivoli From Below the Waterfalls

FRANCIS TOWNE *1781; 20.5 x 39.5 cm (10 x 15½ in); pen and watercolour*

Towne (1739/40–1816) captured this view of Tivoli, near Rome, during a stay in Italy from 1780 to 1781. Kept in albums, his brilliantly coloured drawings were outlined in pen.

POCKET PAINT
This oval pocket box (1900) was manufactured by Winsor and Newton, one of the main paint suppliers in the 19th century. It contains a set of 12 watercolours and was a popular item with artists who wanted to make rough watercolour sketches while out "on location".

LANDSCAPE AT EIN DALIAH BETWEEN MEKNES AND TANGIERS
Eugène Delacroix; 1832; 16 x 9.5 cm (6¼ x 3¾ in); pen and watercolour
Delacroix (1798–1863) was the leader of the 19th-century French Romantic movement in painting. This page is taken from his North African travel diary of 1832, where notes and rapidly made watercolour sketches are mixed together.

ILLUSTRATED CATALOGUE
Winsor and Newton produced illustrated annual catalogues, as comprehensive guides to their artists' supplies. The pages here feature an oval pocket box, shown above, and a small locket box on a ribbon (1850) – worn around an artist's neck.

Satirical images

SATIRE – THE CRITICISM of vice or folly through ridicule – is perhaps one of the most fundamental human impulses to be explored by artists. Satirical drawings can be found in ancient and medieval art, where the features and actions of humans, animals, and deities are exaggerated for comic effect. Watercolour has traditionally been favoured by satirists for individual works of art and for the colouring-in of large print-runs of black and white prints that bring a social or political message to a larger public. The great satirical watercolours were produced from the late 18th century onwards, beginning with the social comedies – often cruel – of Thomas Rowlandson (1756–1827). Political satire, which was even harder-hitting, developed at this time and was typified in France by the work of Honoré Daumier (1810–79).

GEORGE III, AND BONAPARTE

AS

The King of Brobdignag and Gulliver.

GEORGE III AND BONAPARTE (NAPOLEON)
James Gillray; c.1803; 15 x 9.5 cm (6 x 4 in); etching and watercolour
Gillray (1756–1815) was the major British caricaturist of the late 18th and early 19th centuries. His prints focused on the British monarchy, politicians, and foreigners. In particular, he satirized the perpetrators of the Reign of Terror in France after the Revolution in 1789. His etchings were sold from a shop in London, and uncoloured they cost a shilling each; coloured ones were half a crown. The colouring, in watercolour washes, was carried out by a team of women assistants working from a master copy provided by the artist.

SKETCHING A COUNTRY WOMAN
Thomas Rowlandson; 14 x 22.5 cm (5½ x 9 in); pen and watercolour
Rowlandson was an extremely prolific artist, and he had a remarkably fluid drawing style. He drew thousands of humorous watercolours. In this painting, he lampoons the 18th-century fashion for artists to go out into the countryside to sketch rural life. The main woman to the left is stupid and boorish. She does not correspond to the idea, commonly held at the time, of countryfolk being "pure" and unspoilt by the corruption of city life. Even so, the artist, obviously a man of little discrimination, dutifully sketches her. The design was sketched out in pen and then rapidly filled in with watercolour washes.

JOHN BULL and his FAMILY taking leave of the INCOME TAX

JOHN BULL AND HIS FAMILY TAKING LEAVE OF THE INCOME TAX
P. Roberts; 1802; 23.5 x 33.5 cm (9¼ x 13 in); etching with watercolour
This hand-coloured etching is typical of the popular caricatures of Georgian England, in which people were used to illustrate the main issues of the day. John Bull, shown with his family, represents the typical Englishman. The demon symbolizes the hated income tax, which had first been introduced in 1799 to help pay for the war against the French. Here, it is the withdrawal of the tax that is satirized, following the peace with France in 1802. The demon says to John Bull: "Farewell Johnny – Remember me." Bull replies: "... thou'lt be a plague to the Land thou lightest on."

TWO DRINKERS *right*
Honoré Daumier; c.1857–60; 18.5 x 25.5 cm
(7¼ x 10 in); pen, watercolour, and gouache
A prolific draughtsman, Daumier produced many satirical drawings that were reproduced in French newspapers as lithographic prints. His drawings poked fun at French society and Daumier was even imprisoned for his biting satires. This drawing has a tragi-comic tone. The drinkers, clearly well-seasoned alcoholics, wear the over-earnest expressions of semi-drunks in discussion. His deliberately imprecise use of line only adds to the general air of confusion. Daumier had stopped producing newspaper illustrations by this time, so the sale of drawings such as this provided him with an important source of income.

DISCORD
Alexandre Gabriel Decamps; 1833;
41 x 62 cm (16 x 24½ in); watercolour
This was exhibited at the 1833 Paris Salon with a companion drawing, *Perfect Harmony*, which showed monkeys playing music. The titles were a play on words referring to musical harmony, and a highly sarcastic comment on human behaviour. Since classical times, monkeys had been a symbol of evil. In these pictures, their behaviour mimics that of humans – the message being that man is always capable of evil. The number 45 is scratched onto the surface of the painting, a reference to a secret club called *La Société des 45*, of which Decamps (1803–60) was a member.

CARICATURE PORTRAIT OF THE POLITICAL JOURNALIST HENRI ROCHEFORT (1831–1913)
Alfred Le Petit; 1869; 31.5 x 28 cm
(12½ x 10¾ in); black chalk and watercolour
This drawing illustrates how the caricature began to be used as a tool for political satire. Rochefort's features are deliberately exaggerated and his quill pen is portrayed as a "sword". Le Petit (1841–1909) fought for the rights of a free press in Paris, and was often in trouble with the authorities.

SIR CECIL HARCOURT SMITH RECEIVES A DEPUTATION
Sir Max Beerbohm; 1924; 40.5 x 31.5 cm
(16 x 12½ in); pencil and watercolour
This satire pokes fun at the meeting of the lean Director of the Victoria and Albert Museum in London, and a rotund group from the north of England, eager to acquire "culture". In his caricatures, Beerbohm (1872–1956) wished to capture "the peculiarities of the human being ... in the most beautiful manner". His pale washes here are evocative of some of Rowlandson's work.

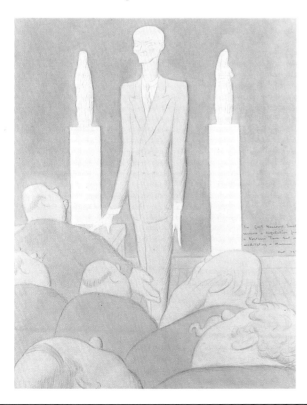

MAGGIE THATCHER
David Lewis; 1992; 29.5 x 21 cm
(11½ x 8 in); pen, ink, and watercolour
Here, the artist stresses Baroness Thatcher's "regal" perception of herself – hence the royal wave and the slight lean forward, as though to an adoring crowd. Her well-known facial features are exaggerated into a rather threatening fixed grin with the lips drawn back over the gums, almost wolf-like. Lewis, a professional caricaturist, uses marker pens for his most rapid sketches, and pen and ink with watercolour for his more finished works.

The British tradition

B ETWEEN ABOUT 1750 and 1850, watercolour was very much associated with British artists. The portability of watercolour equipment meant that it could easily be carried around by artists and travellers increasingly curious about the scenery of Great Britain (pp. 28–29). It became the fashion for young men and women to be proficient in "polite" activities such as dancing, music, and painting in watercolour (pp. 40–41). These amateurs required instruction from professional drawing masters who, in turn, harboured serious ambitions for their own watercolours. By the early 19th century, there were many talented watercolourists in Britain. Masters of the medium, such as Thomas Girtin (1775–1802) and David Cox (1783–1859), rank amongst the finest British painters – as does J.M.W. Turner (1775–1851, pp. 36–37). While the great English landscape artist, John Constable (1776–1837), worked mainly in oils, his powerful watercolours mark a significant contribution to the British tradition.

JOHN CONSTABLE
This is a detail of a drawing by the Irish artist, Daniel Maclise. It shows Constable in 1831, at the age of 55. The drawing was probably made on the occasion of a visit by Constable – a senior figure in the art world – to the Royal Academy Life Schools, where Maclise was a pupil.

Folkestone Harbour with a Rainbow

JOHN CONSTABLE *1833; 12.5 x 21 cm (5 x 8¼ in); watercolour*
This was painted when Constable visited Folkestone to be with his son John Charles – a pupil at a boarding school in the town – who had injured himself. Constable's ability to capture dramatic weather conditions is wonderfully demonstrated here. He found watercolour highly suitable for the rapid portrayal of nature, using it extensively to make preparatory sketches, in particular cloud studies, for his oils.

LOOKING IN DETAIL
The viewer's eye is focused with this central flag, one of few splashes of bold colour in the painting. In the surrounding sky, washes are allowed to run into each other, and parts of the paper are left unpainted, to indicate sunlight bursting through.

KIRKSTALL ABBEY, YORKSHIRE – EVENING
Thomas Girtin; c.1800–01; 31.5 x 52 cm (12½ x 20½ in); watercolour
Turner, Girtin's contemporary, recognized his short-lived rival's genius: "Had Tom lived, I would have starved." Girtin had a huge influence on the watercolour landscape. His strong, varied colours moved away from the more monochromatic (one-colour) approach of many artists at the time, and he pioneered the use of strong cartridge paper. This sort of finished work would have been based on pencil sketches made on the spot and then worked up in the studio. As grandly constructed as any landscape in oils, the semi-transparent washes and delicate effects of watercolour are more suitable for conveying the atmosphere of this scene.

A MONUMENT TO PERPETUATE THE FAME OF BRITISH ARTISTS 1823
This 1830 watercolour (right, detail above), by James Prinsep, was the frontispiece to an album of works by British watercolourists. John Glover has pride of place on the column, while Turner is only halfway up!

LANDSCAPE
John Martin; 1839; 23.5 x 32.5 cm (9¼ x 12¾ in); watercolour
Best known for large, melodramatic paintings of biblical subjects, Martin (1789–1854) was also a highly accomplished watercolourist. Scenes such as this are typical of him, and show a use of fairly rich, dense watercolour. As the century progressed artists tended to prefer richer colours, similar to oils in effect.

THE NIGHT TRAIN
David Cox; 1840s; 28.5 x 38 cm (11¼ x 15 in); watercolour
Cox produced several paintings of this subject. The train shown is probably the night express from Liverpool to Birmingham, where the painter lived. The telling juxtaposition of the horses in the foreground with the train rushing along in the distance is almost certainly intended as a comment on the Industrial Revolution. Cox has used the scratching out of highlights and broken brushwork to give a vivid sense of drama to the picture.

Cotman – a sense of place

JOHN SELL COTMAN (1782–1842) was the most exceptional of the Norwich School of artists, which flourished at the beginning of the 19th century, in eastern England. The flat areas of watercolour that he used in his early paintings gave his designs a semi-abstract appearance. He may have owned several albums of Chinese drawings, and it is possible that he was influenced by the more abstract aspects of Oriental art. His best works are those that he painted during his early 20s; they include the landscapes of Yorkshire, which he produced while he was employed as a drawing master there. From 1831, he started mixing watercolour with rice-paste, producing a rougher and richer paint surface. His work – now seen as innovative – was overlooked for much of the 19th century.

JOHN SELL COTMAN
This was etched by Mrs Dawson Turner of Yarmouth, Norfolk, in 1818, after a drawing by J.P. Davis. Her husband helped to support Cotman financially, commissioning him to illustrate books on churches in Norfolk, and on the scenery in Normandy, France.

Greta Bridge
JOHN SELL COTMAN
c.1807; 22.5 x 33 cm (8¾ x 12¾ in);
pencil and watercolour
This famous British watercolour has a balanced composition and a highly serene atmosphere. It was based on a sketch made in Yorkshire in 1805.

GRETA BRIDGE
John Sell Cotman; 1810; 30 x 50 cm
(11¾ x 19¾ in); pencil and watercolour
A later version of the famous picture of the same title, both paintings probably shared the same preparatory drawing. The colours here are stronger and not as subtle as the original.

DEVIL'S ELBOW, ROKEBY PARK
John Sell Cotman; c.1806–07; 45 x 35 cm (17¾ x 13¾ in); pencil and watercolour
Painted in Rokeby Park, Yorkshire, this scene is close to the location of *Greta Bridge*. The trees are shown here as separate areas of almost flat colour, defined by their outline shapes. Cotman was extraordinarily bold in his use of a high horizon, which allowed him to concentrate on the steep river bank.

**YARMOUTH BEACH
DURING A STORM**
Cotman lived in the coastal town
of Yarmouth from 1812 to 1823. This
etching, of 1821, reflects the general
artistic interest that developed
during the early 1800s in the sea
and its wilder weather conditions.

STORM ON YARMOUTH BEACH
*John Sell Cotman; 1831; 37 x 54 cm
(14½ x 21 in); pen, ink, and watercolour*
By the 1830s, Cotman was using
stronger, less subtle colours than
those of *Greta Bridge* (1807). He
painted the dramatic sky with a dry
brush, and scraped out highlights.

Turner and landscape

JOSEPH MALLORD WILLIAM TURNER (1775–1851) was described by the 19th-century art critic Ruskin as "the most perfect landscape artist that has ever lived". In his thousands of watercolours, Turner showed both technical brilliance and a deep understanding of the medium. He worked rapidly, employing a wide range of techniques. For example, he sometimes manipulated colour with his fingers, rather than a brush, and grew his "eagle claw of a thumbnail" long for scratching out highlights. Blotting paper and breadcrumbs were used for removing colour from certain areas, and partly finished watercolours were immersed in water so that colours would blend into each other. Turner even made use of his saliva – to keep colours moist as he worked with them on the paper.

J.M.W. TURNER
Charles Martin's pencil portrait of Turner was drawn in 1844. Turner began as an architectural draughtsman and print colourer, and became one of the great artists of his age. He was buried, after "lying in state" at his studio, in St. Paul's Cathedral, London.

CRITICAL RESPONSE
This cartoon of Turner (c.1846) refers to widespread criticism of his "free" painting technique. Critics were confused by the artist's bold colours, and the stress that he laid on colour rather than form.

IMAGINARY LANDSCAPE WITH WINDSOR CASTLE
J.M.W. Turner; c.1800; 46 x 74 cm (18 x 29 in);
pencil, watercolour, and bodycolour
This was based on Turner's drawings of Windsor Castle and on others made on his Welsh tours. It is typical of his earlier watercolour work. The relatively narrow colour range and emphasis on tonal balance was characteristic of topographical artists of the time.

View of the Campagna, Italy
J.M.W. TURNER *1819; 26 x 40.5 cm*
(10 x 16 in); pencil and watercolour
Turner's view of the countryside around Rome shows how he used "colour-beginnings" to develop a watercolour. He began to work out the design with almost abstract areas of colour, rather than detailed pencil drawing. Edges were then sharpened to suggest the outlines of hills, and washes that were still wet were brushed into each other to indicate mist and haze.

THE SUN SETTING AMONGST DARK CLOUDS
J.M.W. Turner; c.1825; 27.5 x 47 cm (11 x 18 in); watercolour
This dramatic work shows Turner's range as a water-colourist. The power of nature fascinated him, and this work, with its total lack of human subject-matter, is almost abstract in effect. Black, a colour avoided by most watercolourists, is used here to telling effect.

These cakes of paint give an idea of the "sunset colours" of Turner's palette

The pouch opens like a book, having been made from the binding of an almanac

Watercolour cakes are stuck to the inside of the case

WATERCOLOUR CARRYING CASE
This leather watercolour case – which belonged to Turner – was intended to be convenient to use and easily portable, and he no doubt took it along on his many sketching trips. Turner actually made the watercolour case himself – cleverly using the leather jacket of an almanac.

DEVIL'S BRIDGE, PASS OF ST. GOTHARD
J.M.W. Turner; 1802; 47 x 35 cm (18½ x 13¾ in); pencil, watercolour, and bodycolour
Turner has used scraping out to portray the icy Alpine stream that cascades down the mountainside under the bridge. The bleak, rocky landscape of the upper Alps is depicted with the minimum of colour.

Exhibition works

SEVERAL WATERCOLOUR exhibiting societies were founded in Britain in the early 19th century, due to a growing demand from watercolour artists for proper exhibition venues. Watercolours were now seen as legitimate paintings, rather than mere tinted drawings. In emulation of oil paintings, they became larger, were displayed in gold frames, and used brighter, richer colours – opaque bodycolour was often mixed with transparent watercolour. Glazes of gum arabic were painted over some works to give colours body and depth, rather as varnish is applied to oil paintings.

WATERCOLOURS ON SHOW
The Society of Painters in Watercolours was founded in 1804. This print (reproduced from a watercolour) appeared in a periodical of the time. It shows the Society's 1808 exhibition, at 16, Old Bond Street, London. Many of the works were of considerable size, and all were framed. The effect was intended to rival the annual exhibitions of oil paintings at the Royal Academy.

ORDERS OF MERIT
These medals were awarded to the ar suppliers, Reeves & Son, for their paints. Founded in 1766 in London, their prize-winning cakes of watercolour did much to advance the art (previously, artists had to mix their own paints). The medal above was won at an exhibition in Paris, in 1867; the one on the right, at an 1812 London exhibition.

The Museum Staircase
JEAN-BAPTISTE ISABEY *1817;*
86 x 66 cm (33¾ x 26 in); watercolour

This large painting by Isabey (1767–1855), of a staircase in the Louvre, was exhibited at the 1817 Paris Salon. It marked an important stage in the exhibition of watercolours in France – critics marvelled at its detail and sparkling colour. Watercolour was widely practised in France and gained extra impetus in the 1820s from the landscapes of English artists such as John Constable.

A VILLAGE SNOW SCENE
Robert Hills; 1819; 32.5 x 42.5 cm
(12¾ x 16¾ in); watercolour and bodycolour
Here, snow is depicted by leaving parts of the paper unpainted and "scraping out" the snowflakes (with a sharp point). Hills – a founding member of the Society of Painters in Watercolours – often imitated Old Masters; this scene echoes Rubens's *Barn in Winter* and the work of Brueghel.

STONEHENGE
John Constable; 1836;
38.5 x 59 cm (15¼ x 23¼ in); watercolour
Although Constable (1776–1837) was primarily a painter in oils, he painted several major watercolours towards the end of his life. This dramatic work was exhibited at the Royal Academy in 1836. For the sky, in particular the rainbows, colour has been partially wiped off. The rain effect at the top of the painting has been created by scratching colour on with a stiff brush.

THE THAMES AT ISLEWORTH *right*
John Glover; c.1805–10;
68.5 x 102 cm (27 x 40 in); watercolour
This unfinished drawing shows how the "skeleton" of such a watercolour was laid out. Glover began with tonal washes, often in indigo or Indian red ink, before adding colour. He would later dampen the paper, in order to achieve a softening effect.

ON DISPLAY
This watercolour box was made for the exhibition, "Works of Industry of All Nations" (London, 1851). By this date, the medium was highly popular.

A FRANK ENCAMPMENT IN THE DESERT OF MOUNT SINAI 1842
John Frederick Lewis; 1856; 64.5 x 134 cm (25½ x 52¾ in); watercolour and bodycolour
Lewis's light effects and bright colours influenced the Pre-Raphaelites. He later turned exclusively to oils, and in doing so effectively marked the end of the large exhibition watercolour.

Winsor and Newton box

A genteel pursuit

DURING THE 18TH AND 19TH CENTURIES, an ability to draw became widely regarded as an admirable skill for young ladies and gentlemen. As an activity, it had a similar status to dancing, fencing, or needlework. By the late 18th century, watercolour materials were readily available. For the amateur, painting in watercolours was easier to master, and cheaper, than oils. People often sought tuition from drawing masters or professional artists, whose style they invariably followed. Various instruction manuals were also produced at this time by well-known artists. In 1811, David Cox (pp. 9, 33) published *A Series of Progressive Lessons* and in 1857, John Ruskin (p. 15) wrote *The Elements of Drawing*.

MAN WITH CLAUDE GLASS
This was drawn by Gainsborough
around 1750. This popular
drawing aid reflected the countryside so that it looked like landscape
paintings by old masters.

A LUXURIOUS
ACCESSORY
This decorated
silver water bottle
and brush carrier
was made for
a lady in the
late 18th, or
early 19th,
century.

Two Women Drawing Amidst Classical Ruins

HUBERT ROBERT *1786; 70 x 98 cm (27½ x 38½ in); pen and watercolour*
Here, two ladies are shown lightheartedly sketching the vast ruins of Rome, whilst unknown to them, the spirits of the ancients watch from behind a column. At this time, Rome was an extremely popular subject with amateurs and professionals alike. In 1830, the artist Thomas Uwins wrote with disgust from the ancient city: "What a shoal of amateur artists we have got here!"

PORTABLE CAMERA OBSCURA
This belonged to the 18th-century painter, Sir Joshua Reynolds. It was basically a dark box with a mirror and a lens. The mirror and lens threw light rays from a brightly lit scene in front of the box onto a piece of paper placed inside, so that the artist could trace the scene off. It was popular with amateur artists, as it helped them to draw more accurately.

— Hood, for user's head and shoulders

The base, in which a sheet of drawing paper was placed

The camera folds away to look like a large book

VIEW OF SNOWDON AND LAKE LLANBERIS
Reverend Thomas Gisborne; 1789; 41 x 29 cm (16¼ x 11½ in); watercolour
During the 18th and 19th centuries, a considerable number of clergymen emerged as accomplished watercolourists. Gisborne (1758–1856) was acquainted with the painter Joseph Wright of Derby, and the two men often went on sketching expeditions together to natural beauty spots, such as the Lake District, in the north of England. Gisborne also corresponded with the Reverend William Gilpin, who was the author of various books on good destinations for sketching tours in Britain.

A SKETCHING PARTY IN LEIGH WOODS
Samuel Jackson; c.1830; 44 x 66 cm (17¼ x 25¾ in); watercolour and bodycolour
Jackson (1794–1869) was a successful drawing master who belonged to the Bristol School – a community of professional and amateur artists who lived and worked around England's major south-western city, during the 19th century. This scene shows a sketching class in Leigh Woods, outside Bristol. In his watercolour paintings, Jackson developed a technique using sponging, scratching, and thin glazes of bodycolour.

THE LAMENT OF A DRAWING MASTER
This detail shows the more frivolous side of a sketching expedition – one woman is playing the guitar. By the 19th century, the art teacher tutoring bored young girls had become a literary stereotype. In a story called *The Old Drawing Master*, the teacher Monsieur "La Trobe" laments: "You are all sweet, kind young ladies, you very sweet, and good, ven you not draw, and monche, monche de tops off your crayons, and lose Engee rubbere and mark skies green."

The "mystics"

WILLIAM BLAKE
Blake claimed to have had his first vision – of "a tree filled with angels" – before the age of ten.

THE VISIONARY ART of William Blake (1757–1827), and of other "mystical" artists of the time, was more suited to relatively private media such as watercolour than to grand public statements in oils. Blake painted many watercolours, and also used the medium to colour his prints. He was a highly individual artist, who believed that ideal beauty came from within, without reference to nature. Also a great poet, much of Blake's visual output was produced to illustrate his poems, and his integration of word and image is evocative of medieval illumination (pp. 10–11). His work influenced the "Ancients" – a group centred on the artist, Samuel Palmer, who admired visionary art from the past.

MILDEW BLIGHTING CORN
William Blake; c.1821;
32 x 24.5 cm (12¼ x 9½ in); etching
This plate comes from Blake's own poem, entitled *Europe, A Prophecy*, which revealed his predictions on the fate of Europe. Blake prepared a finely watercoloured edition of this etching for his patron, John Linnell.

ILLUSTRATIONS FOR
NIGHT THOUGHTS
William Blake; c.1795–98;
pen and watercolour
Blake painted over 500 watercolours for Edward Young's book *The Complaint, and the Consolation; or Night Thoughts* (1742–45). As usual, Blake's imagery is complex. His images dominate the text, like a lavish illuminated manuscript.

Jacob's Dream
WILLIAM BLAKE
c.1800–03; 37 x 29 cm
(14½ x 11½ in); watercolour
Here, Blake gives concrete form to a visionary scene. He shows Jacob's dream of God as told in the Old Testament – a vision of God's angels ascending and descending a ladder between heaven and earth.

THE HERDSMAN
Samuel Palmer; c.1855; 52 x 73.5 cm (20½ x 29 in); watercolour
This lyrical work on buff paper is Palmer's idealized vision of the English countryside. Palmer (1805–81) mixed gum and bodycolour to achieve an almost oil-like effect, painting in washes, or, more delicately, with the point of the brush.

PORT STRAGGLIN *above*
Richard Dadd; 1861; 19 x 14
cm (7½ x 5½ in); watercolour
Richard Dadd's eccentric, mystical art was born of madness. From 1844, he was confined to Bedlam Hospital for the murder of his father. He had previously travelled in Greece, Egypt, and the Middle East, and *Port Stragglin* may have been based on some of the stranger sights he had seen there. His technique was delicate, using the pointed tip of the brush.

PHAETON
Gustave Moreau; 1878; 99 x 65 cm
(39 x 25½ in); watercolour and pencil
This lurid work, heightened further by white paint and varnish, was exhibited at the 1878 World Fair in Paris. It shows Phaeton's fall from the sky, as punishment for stealing the chariot of Apollo. As well as making preparatory watercolour sketches for most of his oils, Moreau (1826–98) valued the medium for its own sake. He produced over 400 watercolours. Moreau believed that colours could have a powerful emotional value, and he has used them in this painting to evoke a highly dramatic and tragic scene.

A PRIMITIVE CITY
Edward Calvert; 1822; 7 x 10.5 cm (2¾ x 4 in); pen and watercolour
Like Palmer, Calvert (1799–1883) had been one of the youthful disciples of Blake known as the "Ancients". Calvert based the design of small, exquisite prints and watercolours such as this on Blake's illustrations to Thorton's *Virgil*. He conjures up, almost as in an illuminated manuscript, an innocent, imaginary world of female beauty and plentiful nature.

IN DETAIL
The donkey and his master lead the procession into the city laden with produce. Calvert's water-colour technique is closely based on Palmer's earlier work. Pen outlines play an important part, and give an almost speckled effect.

Book illustrations

COLOUR BOOK ILLUSTRATION originating
from watercolour artwork is a relatively new
art form. It grew out of the development of
sophisticated colour printing techniques,
during the second half of the 19th century.
Before this, printers had not been able to
reproduce original watercolours accurately.
In the 18th century, the initial artwork for
colour engraving had to be designed in
black and white – the colour was added
as a later process. The traditional use of
watercolour for hand-colouring black
and white prints (p. 30) made it a natural
medium for illustrators. The late 19th and
early 20th centuries became the golden age
of children's book illustration in England.
Certain highly popular illustrators gained
celebrity status, and the major London
publishing companies competed with
their top children's artists.

GIRL AND TWO BABIES
Kate Greenaway; c.1870s; 18 x 12 cm (7¼ x 4¼ in); pen and watercolour
Greenaway's illustrations of children in 18th-century dress – partly of her own
invention – were extremely popular in late Victorian England. Kate Greenaway
(1846–1901) started out doing drawings for cards and children's magazines. In
1870, the colour printer Edmund Evans commissioned her to illustrate books of
her own poems. Evans used several coloured printing blocks – red, flesh tint,
blue, and yellow – to reproduce the quality of the original watercolours.

CINDERELLA
*Artist unknown; c.1876; 14.5 x
14.5 cm (5½ x 5½ in); watercolour*
Fairy stories were a popular
choice for mass-produced
books. This book, featuring
Cinderella and *Little Red
Riding Hood*, has surprise
pictures hidden under
movable flaps.

OLIVER TWIST *right*
*George Cruikshank; 1866;
10 x 9.5 cm (4 x 3¾ in);
pencil and watercolour*
Cruikshank began as a
political cartoonist, and
later became the first artist
to illustrate children's books
humorously. He was the
ideal collaborator for Charles
Dickens, whose characters
were often caricatures.

WUTHERING HEIGHTS
*Edmund Dulac; 1905;
22 x 16.5 cm (8½ x 6½ in);
watercolour*
Dulac (1882–1953) trained
in Paris as a painter before
becoming an illustrator.
In his own words, he was
"fascinated by pigment
and colour", and was also
greatly influenced by Art
Nouveau (a highly ornate
style that spread across
Europe and America in
the 1890s). He used colour
almost entirely for its
decorative effect, working
carefully from pencil-
drawn foundations. This
is part of a series of watercolours that Dulac was
commissioned to produce
to illustrate a complete set
of novels by the Brontës.

WINNIE-THE-POOH
Ernest H. Shepard; 1926; pen and watercolour
Shepard (1879–1976) was one of the most successful illustrators from the inter-war years; his images of Pooh are better known than A.A. Milne's stories. Shepard gave his Pooh illustrations (first published in 1926) a new wash in 1973–74.

TREASURE ISLAND
Salomon van Abbé; 1948; 37.5 x 27 cm (14¼ x 10½ in); pencil and watercolour
This is one of several drawings made for a 1948 edition of Robert Louis Stevenson's novel, which was first published in 1883. A scene of action, its main characters are shown in period costume. Conventional in style, it indicates the continuing demand for traditional watercolour illustrations in classic children's books.

THUMBELINA
Joan Charleton; 1960; 30 x 40 cm (11¾ x 15¾ in); pen and watercolour
This illustrates Hans Christian Andersen's 19th-century fairy tale about Thumbelina, the miniature child. Although probably reproduced with modern printing techniques, in which a watercolour is "read photographically", the finished result is stylistically similar to that of early colour illustrations such as *Cinderella* (p. 44). A commercial rather than a "fine art" illustration, it is designed to appeal to a wide range of children.

THUMBELINA ENLARGED
Although Thumbelina is tiny, the illustrator turns the other figures (above) to look at her, making her central to the story, and to the picture.

POP-UP RUPERT
This pop-up annual, featuring Rupert the Bear, was published by the *Daily Express* newspaper in 1931. The *Daily Express* Rupert annuals became a much-loved institution.

Rupert is shown in his original clothes: blue jumper, grey-check trousers, and scarf

RUPERT THE BEAR
Mary Tourtel; 1931; watercolour
Rupert was created in 1920 by the children's illustrator Mary Tourtel, as a comic strip for *The Daily Express*. Almost immediately, Rupert memorabilia and pop-up annuals, such as this, were produced in response to his popularity. Tourtel retired in 1936, and has since been replaced by several generations of illustrators. In the 1970s and '80s, animated cartoons were made about Rupert and his friends. An effort has been made to keep Rupert true in his essential features and colours to Tourtel's original watercolours.

The Pre-Raphaelites

DANTE GABRIEL ROSSETTI (1828–82), Sir John Everett Millais (1829–96), and William Holman Hunt (1827–1910) formed the Pre-Raphaelite Brotherhood in 1848. They aspired to a "pure" style that they felt existed prior to the Italian artist, Raphael (1483–1520). Medieval and literary themes were stressed, and in covering these in their watercolours, they moved away from typical water-colour subjects, such as landscape. They favoured areas of flat, vivid colour and extremely fine, sharply focused details, which they picked out with bodycolour.

A FAMILY PORTRAIT
Dante Gabriel Rossetti is on the extreme left of this 1863 family photograph.

HORATIO DISCOVERING THE MADNESS OF OPHELIA
Dante Gabriel Rossetti; 1864;
39.5 x 29 cm (15½ x 11½ in); watercolour and bodycolour
Until 1860, Rossetti worked primarily in watercolour. This painting has a two-dimensional quality, emphasized by the shields in the background that are brought forward by their bold colours. The tragic suicide of Ophelia, in Shakespeare's *Hamlet*, was echoed in Rossetti's own life – his wife, Elizabeth Siddal, died from an overdose of the drug, laudanum.

THE MILL ON THE THAMES AT MAPLEDURHAM
George Price Boyce; 1860; 27.5 x 57 cm (10¾ x 22¼ in); watercolour
An architect by training, Boyce (1826–97) often filled his landscape paintings either with trees, or with buildings, as he has done here. He achieved his brilliant tones and sharp details, which were so typical of Pre-Raphaelite landscapes, by preparing his paper first with a layer of gum.

CHAFFINCH NEST AND MAY BLOSSOM
William Henry Hunt; c.1845; 24.5 x 37.5 cm
(9½ x 14¾ in); watercolour and bodycolour
Hunt's watercolours encouraged many artists to paint in bodycolour, and were avidly collected by the Victorian public. He created luminous effects with a hard surface of gum mixed with Chinese white, onto which he then painted pure watercolour.

HIGHLIGHTED DETAIL
Hunt used Chinese white for highlights, and for reflected light – here, he mixed pigments into the white to make the eggs rich in tone, and opaque in colour.

Phyllis and Demophoön
SIR EDWARD COLEY BURNE-JONES
1870; 91.5 x 46 cm (36 x 18 in); watercolour and bodycolour

Burne-Jones (1833–98) took this subject from *Heroides*, by the Roman writer, Ovid. In the story, Demophoön's lover, Phyllis, is changed into an almond tree. Burne-Jones' figures echoed those of the 15th-century Florentine artist, Sandro Botticelli. Some of the criticism levelled at this picture when it was first shown was due to the nudity of the male figure.

SIR EDWARD COLEY BURNE-JONES
Along with William Morris (pp. 48–49), Burne-Jones headed the second wave of Pre-Raphaelitism. Shown here in 1890, he designed items such as wallpapers and tapestries for the firm of Morris, Marshall, Faulkner and Co.

THE PAINTER'S PLEASURE
*Simeon Solomon; 1861; 25.5 x 33 cm (10 x 13 in);
watercolour and bodycolour*
This painting shows an episode in the life of an imaginary Venetian painter of the Renaissance. Solomon (1840–1905) used a rich watercolour technique, similar to Rossetti's, in this work. The paint (mainly bodycolour) was applied fairly dry over monochrome (one-colour) underpainting and then scraped out with a knife to create highlights. A gum arabic varnish was also applied to the painting.

The flatness of *Phyllis and Demophoön* makes it seem almost like a rich tapestry

THE HOLY CITY *right*
*William Holman Hunt; c.1854; 19.5 x 34.5 cm
(7½ x 13½ in); watercolour and bodycolour*
This painting of Jerusalem is the result of one of Hunt's trips to Egypt and Palestine, during which he painted largely in watercolours. His Eastern watercolours are most notable for their deep colours, particularly indigo and purple.

A company of craftsmen

W ILLIAM MORRIS (1834–96) was a major figure in the
second wave of Pre-Raphaelitism (pp. 46–47). His talent was
for design and pattern, and the firm that he founded in 1861 –
Morris, Marshall, Faulkner and Company – had London show-
rooms that sold furniture, tapestries, metalwork, stained glass,
jewellery, wallpaper, and fabrics. He employed various artists
to produce beautifully detailed watercolours as preparatory
designs. Like the other
Pre-Raphaelites, the style
and approach of his work
looked back to simpler
times. Reacting against
the industrialization of
Victorian society, he
based his company
on a Medieval guild
of skilled craftsmen,
making high-quality
items by hand.

PORTRAIT OF WILLIAM MORRIS
Cosmo Rowe; c.1895; 39 x 29 cm (15 x 11 in); oil on canvas
Morris was born in north London, the son of a
wealthy broker. After Oxford University, where he
met Burne-Jones (p. 47), he turned to architecture,
and then to painting, before
starting his company.

DESIGN FOR "TRELLIS" WALLPAPER
1862; 66 x 58.5 cm (26 x 23 in); watercolour and pencil
This was the first of 70 wallpaper designs from Morris's
workshop. It was derived from a wooden trellis at his
home, the Red House at Bexleyheath, south-east of
London. Designs were often the work of a number of
people; here the birds were drawn by Philip Webb.

**DESIGN FOR
"TULIP" FABRIC** *right*
*1875; 45.5 x 25.5 cm (18 x
10 in); watercolour and pencil*
Watercolour was
ideal for working
out designs, rapidly
producing broad washes
of colour, through which
pencil sketches could
still be seen.

Wooden printing block

*Cotton printed with
"Tulip" design*

*The basic pencil design is
still clearly visible beneath
the washes of watercolour*

"TULIP" PRINTING BLOCK AND "TULIP" DESIGN FABRIC *left*
Once finalized, the design was cut out of a wooden block –
usually pear wood. Here, an original block (32 x 24 cm / 12
x 9 in) and printed fabric are shown. To print onto fabric,
dye was applied to the block by hand, as Morris stressed
traditional methods. One colour was printed at a time.

Design for the "Pomona" Tapestry

WILLIAM MORRIS & SIR EDWARD BURNE-JONES

c.1884; 40 x 30 cm (15¾ x 11¾ in); watercolour

Pomona was a Roman goddess of *poma*, the Latin word for "fruits". The figure of Pomona was drawn by Burne-Jones. Morris added her costume, the background, the decorative border, and the scrolls of text. Morris usually worked with collaborators on his tapestry designs.

THE NATURAL WORLD
This detail is taken from the bottom left of the design. Morris's love of all kinds of natural forms is once again evident here. The borders and background of this watercolour are almost reminiscent of a medieval "herbal" (pp. 14–15) in the detail with which the flowers and leaves have been painted.

MEDIEVAL VALUES
As this design shows, the work of Morris and his associates was inspired by the intricate details and rich colours of the art of the late Middle Ages. Morris sought to recreate a more innocent, natural age: "To turn our chamber walls into the green woods of the leafy month of June, populous of bird and beast; or a summer garden with man and maid playing round a fountain, or a solemn procession of the mythical warriors and heroes of old; that surely was worth the trouble of doing."

The watercolour paint effectively conveys both deep shadows and sunlit highlights on this border of grapes

A PORTRAIT OF POMONA
The face of Pomona, drawn by Burne-Jones, has the look of many of the women in paintings by the Pre-Raphaelites (pp. 46–47). As with Burne-Jones' other work (p. 47), it also shows similarities to the paintings of Botticelli. The watercolour has been used so that it gives Pomona's skin a convincing ivory translucence, rather like some of the effects achieved by earlier miniature painters (pp. 22–23).

The way in which the scroll has been painted gives a strong three-dimensional feel

Impressionism

WOMAN OF ALGIERS
Eugène Delacroix;
1832; 19.5 x 13 cm
(7½ x 5 in); watercolour
A great influence on
the Impressionists,
Delacroix filled his
travel journals with
outdoor studies.

Watercolour was frequently used by the Impressionists, whose style tended to suppress outline in favour of brilliant areas of colour. The group's preoccupations with light effects, and with painting out of doors, were interests that were well suited to watercolour technique. The first Impressionist exhibition held in Paris, in 1874, signified a break with classical and historical subjects, which were traditionally executed in oils. While oil painting did remain the central activity of the Impressionists, watercolours were included in all eight of their group exhibitions. During the economic depressions of the 1880s, watercolours rather than oil paintings were often produced in response to dealers' demands for cheaper work.

PORTRAIT OF BERTHE MORISOT
Edouard Manet; 1874; 20.5 x 16.5 cm (8 x 6½ in); watercolour
Manet's extremely fluid manner of painting in watercolour is clearly in evidence. Forms are painted, rather than drawn, and thin washes are allowed to run into one another over the ivory paper. The painting exudes a feeling of confidence that reflects how at ease Manet (1832–83) was with the paint. Morisot married Manet's younger brother Eugène. Here, she wears black, in mourning for her father who had died that year.

CARRIAGE IN THE BOIS DE BOULOGNE *left*
Berthe Morisot; 1889; 25 x 22.5 cm (10 x 8¾ in); watercolour
Most of the watercolours by Morisot (1841–95) dealt with female family members. However, here she evokes the atmosphere and light of a fashionable area of Paris, using highly diluted washes of colour to give the subtlest suggestion of shape, volume, and light. The choice of contemporary subject matter is typical of an Impressionist. Unlike the art that went before it, Impressionism sought to portray modern life and society, rather than historical, mythological, or religious subjects.

Girl in a Field with Turkeys
CAMILLE PISSARRO
1885; 64 x 20 cm (25¼ x 7¾ in); gouache on silk fan
Pissarro's interest in painting fans was strongly stimulated by the contemporary fascination with Japanese art. Painted on silk, the gouache has been laid on heavily so that the fan is not transparent. Pissarro (1831–1903) experimented with a number of painting styles throughout his career, concentrating in particular on watercolour painting during the 1880s.

LANDSCAPE NEAR LA CÔTE-SAINT-ANDRÉ (DAUPHINÉ)
*Johan Barthold Jongkind; 1880; 14 x 23 cm (5½ x 9¼ in);
watercolour and bodycolour over black chalk*
Jongkind was an important precursor of Impressionism,
and his broad, sweeping landscapes influenced artists
such as the young Monet in the early 1860s. A group
of paintings composed after 1863 was later described
by the theorist Paul Signac as "... the finest series of
watercolours in the world." Jongkind was a prolific
watercolourist, who enjoyed painting the coasts
of France and Holland. His vigorous, broken touch
is clear in works such as this view
of south-eastern France.

GONDOLIERS AT VENICE
*Jean-Louis-Ernest
Meissonier; 1870; 29 x 41.5 cm
(11¼ x 16¼ in); pencil,
watercolour, and gouache*
Meissonier shared many of
the Impressionists' artistic
interests, although he was
not strictly a member of
their group. He was, like
them, preoccupied by the
portrayal of light. An
accomplished watercolour
painter, he recalled, "I no
longer like painting in oils;
nothing is as agreeable
as watercolour."

TAHITIAN LANDSCAPE
*Paul Gauguin; 19 x 30 cm
(7½ x 11¾ in); watercolour*
This richly coloured sketch
is taken from *Noa Noa*,
Gauguin's journal of
his first voyage to
Tahiti, in 1891. Here,
Gauguin (1848–1903)
chose watercolour
to express his
intense reaction
to the South
Pacific.

Cézanne – art and light

PAUL CÉZANNE (1839–1906), one of the most influential painters of the 19th century, pointed the way forwards from Impressionism towards Abstraction (pp. 50, 60). Watercolour was just as important to him as oils – his many watercolours were rarely related to his oil paintings, and developed in parallel. The medium suited his love of colour and light, and he was increasingly drawn to its transparency, using much less opaque colour in his later work. His distinctive approach included allowing one colour to dry before laying a second on top – he seldom let colours run together. This gave Cézanne's watercolours a glow, as one colour shone up through another.

MAN WEARING A STRAW HAT
*Paul Cézanne; 1906; 48 x 31.5 cm
(19 x 12½ in); pencil and watercolour*
In his late watercolours, such as this one, Cézanne achieves a striking luminous quality. Colour is laid over the white paper surface, which shines through and enhances the sense of light playing over the surfaces.

THE THREE BATHERS
*Paul Cézanne; 1874–75;
11.5 x 12.5 cm (4½ x 5 in);
pencil, watercolour, and gouache*
Cézanne's bathers are often seen as an attempt to recreate the classical idea – revived in the Renaissance – of beauty in nature. The untidy outlines and frenzied application of colour, however, are far removed from classical balance and calm.

MARKS OF TIME
White paint has been used to "heighten" (highlight) the bodies. These white patches have been discoloured by oxidization.

THE MOUNTAIN OF SAINTE-VICTOIRE
*Paul Cézanne; 1885-87; 31.5 x 47.5 cm
(12½ x 18¾ in); pencil and watercolour*
With just a few inspired strokes of colour, Cézanne manages to convey the mighty form of the mountain that overlooks Aix-en-Provence, and is the main landmark of this region. He painted it many times, and this view is from the south-west, looking over the valley of the River Arc.

Still Life with Apples, Bottle and Chairback

PAUL CÉZANNE

1902–06; 44.5 x 59 cm (17½ x 23¼ in); pencil and watercolour

As Cézanne was a slow, careful worker, still lifes would have provided him with the ideal material. However, his still lifes have an energy not normally associated with such subject-matter. Forms seem to balance precariously on one another and spatial relationships are often slightly ambiguous. It is as though the whole composition is about to rearrange itself.

The paint is applied in short strokes

Layers of overlapping paint can be seen

An initial pencil sketch creates the basic form

SUBTLE BRUSHSTROKES
This detail shows the subtlety of Cézanne's touch, and how he laid colour over a framework of preliminary underdrawing. A patchwork of semi-transparent colours is laid over this framework, almost like a screen on which the colours seem to vibrate.

The nude in watercolour

THE UNCLOTHED HUMAN BODY has been portrayed in Western art since classical times. To the ancient Greeks and Romans, it represented the perfection of their gods, while, during the Middle Ages, nakedness spelled human guilt – Adam and Eve's expulsion from Paradise. For watercolour artists, the nude offers a chance to use the medium to stunning effect. Watercolour requires rapid execution, and a few swift strokes can capture the basic lines of the body in a way that is both graceful and dramatic. It is also an ideal medium for depicting the soft sheen of skin – by leaving areas of paper unpainted, or by letting the paper shine through its transparent washes.

PAINTING UNDER DIFFICULTIES
Thomas Rowlandson; date unknown;
22 x 28.5 cm (8½ x 11¼ in); pen and watercolour
Rowlandson (1756–1827) here pokes fun at the tradition of male artists drawing and painting from naked female models. Caught in one woman's embrace, the artist is so distracted that he finds it difficult to paint. The models are shown as fat-bellied and voluptuous, according to the fashion of the time.

THE TWO FRIENDS
Jules-Robert Auguste; c.1820; 22.5 x 26 cm
(9 x 10¼ in); watercolour and gouache
One of several Auguste paintings of black and white nudes together, this was undoubtedly meant to appeal to collectors of mild erotica. It is typical of his watercolours in being highly finished and coated with gum arabic varnish to give it an extra richness.

Odalisque

JEAN AUGUSTE DOMINIQUE INGRES *1864;*
34.5 x 23.5 cm (13½ x 9¼ in); watercolour
This exotic work shows an odalisque – an Eastern slave or concubine – in a Turkish bath. It is a reworking of earlier oil paintings produced by Ingres (1780–1867). The French artist has used watercolour to give these nudes the sensual quality that appeared in his oils of the same subjects. The watercolour has lent soft highlights to the smooth skin of the main nude – which is painted with the same kind of idealization evident in much of Ingres' work.

Neptune

AUGUSTE RODIN *1890;
32.5 x 24.5 cm (12¾ x 9½ in);
pencil and watercolour*

Rodin produced a huge
number of rapidly executed
pencil drawings of nudes,
and to many of these studies
he added watercolour wash.
He used the paint sparingly,
but achieved the maximum
effect. In this drawing of
the Roman god of water, the
dark watercolour added for
the hair and beard lends a
softness that contrasts with
the spare lines of the body.

AUGUSTE RODIN (1840–1917)
Rodin was principally a sculptor,
and his figures have a dynamism
far removed from the frozen
lifelessness of much "academic"
sculpture. Also a prolific draughtsman, the French artist's frank,
unconventional drawings of nudes
had a considerable influence on
artists as diverse as Gustav
Klimt and Henri Matisse.

Modern uses of the medium

ELEMENTS OF DESIGN
This house is a detail from a chintz design by Charles Voysey (see below). Voysey was an architect, famous for designing houses in this style. The watercolour is used to provide general washes of colour, and to pick out small, vivid details.

In the 20th century, watercolour's versatility has ensured that it has had many applications outside the world of "fine art". It has often been used in advertising, to convey a specific atmosphere – the railway poster on p. 57 uses the gentle associations of traditional watercolour landscape painting to conjure up an idyllic rural image. Despite the growing role of computers in design, watercolour is still of particular value in the preparatory stages of designing all kinds of projects – from stage sets to high fashion. For designers, working with such a fluid medium makes them feel more involved in the act of creation, and its cheapness and accessibility add to its appeal. For prospective clients, or the public, the bright, sparkling qualities of watercolour make it instantly attractive. These pages show how watercolour continues to fulfil its varied potential.

DESIGN FOR A NURSERY CHINTZ
Charles Voysey; 1929; 49 x 59 cm (19¼ x 23¼ in); pen, pencil, and watercolour

This faint drawing is a caricature of Voysey's brother, who was a Unitarian minister

This watercolour illustrates the popular nursery rhyme, *The House That Jack Built*. It is a preparatory design for a printed cotton fabric intended for use in a nursery. The paint has been applied with skill, and the light, bright colours that can be achieved with watercolour convey this nursery theme particularly well. Voysey (1857–1941) was an influential domestic architect who also designed furniture, fabrics, and wallpapers, in the same kind of tradition as William Morris (pp. 48–49). As in much of Morris's work, the detailed plants and animals are reminiscent of medieval manuscripts (pp. 10–13).

Model for *Le Comte Ory* ("Count Ory")

OLIVER MESSEL *1954; 61 x 91 cm (24 x 36 in); model painted in watercolour*
This model is a set design for a 1954 production of Rossini's opera of 1823. Some of the details for the medieval setting, for example on the castle, were adapted from medieval tapestries. The story concerns a Countess and her companion who are left behind in a castle when their men go off to the Crusades. Count Ory and his men enter the castle disguised as nuns, but the crusaders return and sort the situation out. Once again, watercolour shows its ability to convey both broad scenic effects and finer details such as animals and foliage.

**DESIGN FOR THE CORNICHE
MOSQUE, JEDDAH, SAUDI ARABIA**
*Abdel Wahed El-Wakil (architect) and Edwin Venn (artist);
1989; 25 x 30 cm (9¾ x 11¾ in); watercolour and pencil*
El-Wakil, an Egyptian architect, designed the Corniche Mosque
as part of a "beautification" programme for Jeddah. It is set on
an isolated sand dune above a coral reef. Watercolour is
particularly suitable for illustrating buildings because the lines
of a basic design can remain visible beneath the washes. It is an
appealing way of presenting designs to clients – El-Wakil has
commissioned Venn to paint many of his building designs.

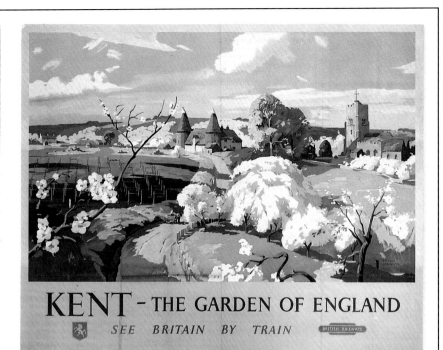

KENT - THE GARDEN OF ENGLAND
SEE BRITAIN BY TRAIN BRITISH RAILWAYS

RAILWAY POSTER
Frank Sherwin; c.1955; 16 x 19.5 cm (40 x 50 in); gouache
The railway posters designed by commercial artist Frank Sherwin before and after World
War II were highly successful. Many 20th-century British Railways posters worked so well
because they celebrated the countryside through which trains travelled, not the trains
themselves. Here, the popular watercolour landscape is used to evoke an idealized English
scene. This was Sherwin's favourite medium, and
many of his watercolours were reproduced
by card manufacturers.

This cloak, worn by the witch in
Hansel and Gretel, shows the
children that she has eaten!

**CLOAK DESIGN FOR
*HANSEL AND GRETEL***
*Terry Frances Parr (designer)
and Roger A. Oakes (painter);
1990; water-soluble paints on fabric*
This costume was created for
a production of Humperdinck's
opera. It is painted with water-
soluble paints that become fixed
to the fabric when it is ironed.

FASHION DESIGN
*Emma Mandell-Lynn; 1992;
42 x 29½ cm (16½ x 11½ in); watercolour*
Like many clothes designers, Mandell-Lynn
works out her designs in watercolour. She often
builds up a design in cut-out pieces of paper
painted in watercolour and then stuck together.
Gouache, with its strong colouring, is used for
details and finished designs, while transparent
colour is employed for spontaneous ideas.

**THE PERFECT
MEDIUM**
Mandell-Lynn
finds water-
colour fast,
simple to use,
fluid, and
easy on the
eye. She feels
that it is ideal
for "getting a
whole look
across".

Expressionism

RUSSIAN PRISONER OF WAR
*Egon Schiele; 1916; 44 x 31 cm
(17¼ x 12 in); pencil and gouache*
Schiele (1890–1918) "coloured in"
this drawing with gouache. Line
was an important aspect
of his work.

THE EXPRESSIONISTS' watercolours contradict any reputation that the medium may have for being "safe" or purely descriptive. The main purpose of art for the Expressionists was to express emotion, and they set out to do this by exaggerating line, colour, and form. This approach was directly opposed to the Impressionists (pp. 40–41), and their strong emphasis on imitating nature. Although there was a parallel movement in France (Fauvism), Germany became the centre of Expressionism, and two main groups were formed there. The first was called *Die Brücke* ("The Bridge"), and included Emil Nolde (1867–1956). Founded in Dresden in 1905, it lasted until 1913. The second was *Der Blaue Reiter* ("The Blue Rider"). This was formed in Munich and the Germans, Franz Marc (1880–1916) and August Macke (1887–1914), were prominent members.

TWO BLUE HORSES IN FRONT OF A RED ROCK
Franz Marc; 1913; 14 x 9 cm (5½ x 3½ in); tempera
Marc, who sent this as a postcard to the Russian artist Kandinsky (p. 60), believed in colour's power of expression. He wrote of his unusual choice of colours: "Blue is the male principle ... Red is matter, brutal and heavy ..."

ST. GERMAIN, NEAR TUNIS
August Macke; 1914; 26 x 21 cm (10¼ x 8¼ in); watercolour
Macke painted this on a visit to Tunisia with the artist Paul Klee (p. 61). As a member of *Der Blaue Reiter*, Macke was especially interested in colour and form. In this painting, he showed the distant Tunisian mountain as blue pyramids. The effect was achieved by his application of three dominant, overlapping blue washes.

THE COUPLE
George Grosz; c.1922–24; 57.5 x 46 cm (22½ x 18 in); watercolour and ink
This sums up political satirist Grosz's contempt for 1920s Germany. An Expressionist in intensity of feeling, his use of watercolour was extremely informed and aided his bitter attacks on contemporary German society.

Sunflowers
EMIL NOLDE
c.1937; 27 x 23 cm (10½ x 9 in); watercolour
Although a member of *Die Brücke*, and an exhibitor with *Der Blaue Reiter*, Nolde had an extremely individual approach to his art. This is particularly true of his watercolour technique. He used a thick, highly absorbent rice paper, soaking it in water so that, when he applied paint, the colours saturated the page – "floating" into one another. In some of his paintings, the paper became so saturated that the picture was also visible on the reverse, making the two sides indistinguishable. Nolde even signed some of his watercolours on both the front and the back.

FLOWING COLOUR

Nolde's "wet-on-wet" technique of painting gives his subject-matter a striking spontaneity. It is as if he has just lifted his brush from the paper. He has allowed the brilliant blue of the background to flow onto the edges of the flowers and leaves, helping to define the darker tips of the flowers' petals.

VIBRANT WATERCOLOURS

Despite their vivid colouring, Nolde's watercolours of flowers are exceptional in their tranquillity. Expressionists such as Nolde are usually associated with more emotionally charged subjects. Much of Nolde's work was religious, and has been described as possessing a "particularly ferocious quality".

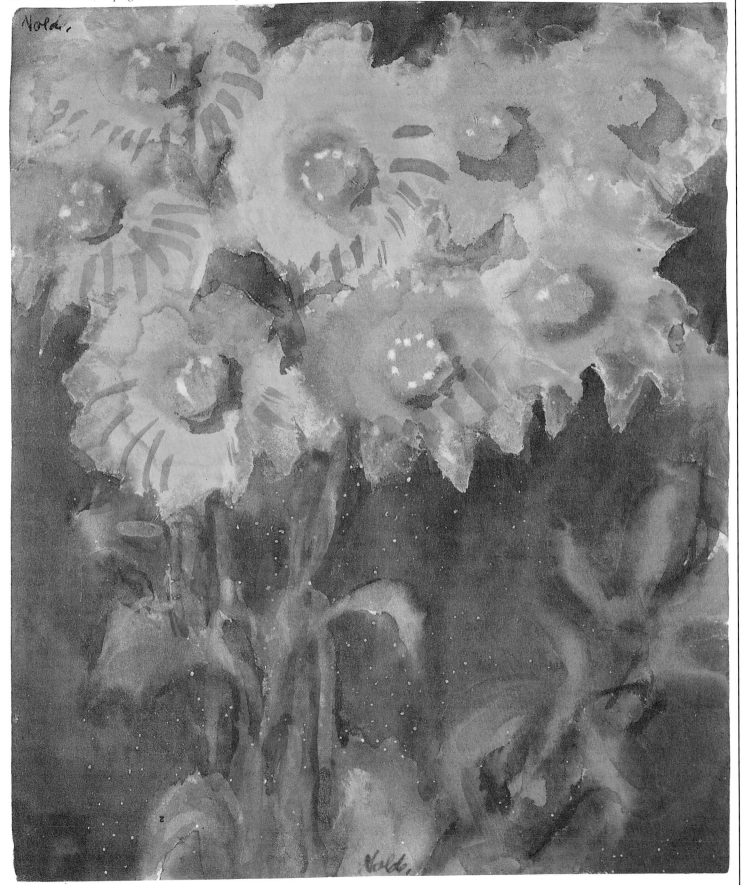

Into the abstract world

THE FIRST TEN YEARS of the 20th century saw a move in Western art away from the realism that had dominated since the 15th and 16th centuries, towards an approach loosely labelled "Abstraction". The advance of photography, invented in the mid-19th century, seemed to have ended the quest to represent reality. Artists began to explore form and colour for their own sake, rather than depict recognizable subjects, and it was movements such as Cubism and Expressionism (pp. 58–59) that paved the way. Some of the most significant 20th-century artists have used abstract images, and have found the fluid nature of watercolour ideal for producing these kinds of forms. This was evident even in the 19th century, in the freer watercolours of Turner and Cézanne (pp. 36–37, 52–53). By the 20th century, abstract artists had found new ways of using watercolour – for example, Picasso's harsh brushwork in *Head of a Woman* (below, left). Because of the medium's immediacy – any errors are difficult to correct – it is perfect for artists exploring basic shapes and colours.

HINEIN
*Wassily Kandinsky; 1928;
38.5 x 26.5 cm (15 x 10½ in); watercolour*
The Russian artist, Kandinsky (1866–1944), often sprayed watercolour paint onto the paper with an atomizer or blow-pipe, as he has in this painting. Like many abstract artists, he experimented with mixing different media – for example, splattering the surface of a watercolour with ink to add texture and depth.

HEAD OF A WOMAN
*Pablo Picasso; 1909;
30.5 x 23.5 cm (12 x 9 in);
watercolour and gouache*
This is one of Picasso's early Cubist works – reality is fragmented so that objects and people are seen from different points of view at the same time. The sharp, angular strokes create the effect of pencil or crayon, unlike the fluid brushwork seen in most watercolours. He has used gradations of colour, and the washes have been applied over a strong linear "scaffolding".

PABLO PICASSO (1881–1973)
Picasso is considered to be one of the 20th century's most important artists. Born in Spain, he spent most of his life in France. With Georges Braque, he was a founder member of the early 20th-century group, the Cubists, and later became involved with Surrealism. Although much of his art was semi-abstract, it remained dominated by the human figure.

The Polychrome Flower
FERNAND LÉGER *1937;
42 x 60 cm (16½ x 23½ in); gouache*
Much of Léger's work divorces objects from their normal surroundings. Here, it is a starfish-shaped flower, painted in the strong colours possible with gouache. Léger (1881–1955) made increasing use of watercolour, especially to give planes of flat colour that contrasted well with his dynamic shapes and vibrant colour-schemes.

Still Life with Apple
PAUL KLEE *1932; 25 x 31 cm*
(9¾ x 12¼ in); watercolour
The paintings of the Swiss
artist, Klee (1879–1940),
cannot really be linked with
any specific movement. He
often worked in watercolour,
using the medium with great
delicacy. In various works,
he combined watercolour
with other media, even with
oils. Lines took a central role
in his paintings – he wrote of
"taking a line for a walk".

NORTHWEST DRIFT
Mark Tobey; 1958; 113.5 x 90.5 cm
(44¾ x 35½ in); tempera and gouache
Born in Wisconsin, U.S.A., Tobey
(1890–1976) is known as a pioneer
of Abstract Expressionism. In
Northwest Drift, the quality of the
paint conveys a sense of the ocean –
for much of his life, Tobey lived in
Seattle, on America's Pacific coast.

UNTITLED
Anish Kapoor; 1988; 56 x 56 cm (22 x 22 in); gouache
Many artists have found watercolour or gouache ideal
for analysing the nature of colour. Kapoor's colours
are limited, but each is highly significant. The Indian-
born artist (b. 1954) uses colour to paint the "interior ...
of me". Brown washes often form a basis for his work,
and red may represent bodily organs, as it does here.

Glossary

Aquatint A type of etching that reproduces the wash effects of watercolour.

Bodycolour Watercolour that has been thickened and made opaque by adding lead white. From the 19th century, Chinese white was used instead. (See also Gouache.)

Brushes Watercolour brushes were traditionally made from sable or squirrel hair. These are still used today, as is polyester. Good brushes must come to a fine point when wet, to allow detailed working of the paint.

Medieval manuscripts, precursors of modern watercolours, were painted in bodycolour on parchment or vellum. Glair was used as a binding agent.

Cakes From the late 18th century, watercolours were manufactured in cake form. Honey was added to prevent the paint from drying out.

Chinese white Zinc oxide. Used as a white pigment to make watercolour opaque.

Engraving A method of printmaking. Lines are cut into a copper plate with a tool called a burin. When this plate is inked up, ink is held in the incised lines, and it is these lines that come out in the print.

Etching A process similar to engraving, except that the etcher draws on a gum- or wax-covered plate, using a metal point. The etched plate is placed in acid, which eats into the plate where it has been exposed by the metal point.

Glair A binding agent made of egg white, used particularly in medieval manuscripts. It was superseded by gum arabic.

An 1865 Winsor and Newton box for storing watercolour paints.

Glaze A thin layer of gum arabic applied over a watercolour. This gives underlying colours an added richness and brilliance.

Gouache Watercolour that either: 1) has a high concentration of coloured pigment, *or* 2) is mixed with white pigment or chalks to which gum or honey have been added. A gouache colour is strong, bright, and opaque, and totally obscures the painting surface underneath. The term is often used loosely instead of bodycolour.

Ground A preparatory surface, consisting of either: 1) Chinese white, used to heighten the brilliance of colours laid over the top, *or* 2) dark washes, used to give various tonal qualities to overlaid paint.

Gum arabic The normal binding agent used in watercolour, which makes the paint adhere to the paper. It is a vegetable gum derived from the acacia tree, and, unlike other resins, is soluble in water. Gum arabic is ground up and mixed with pigments to make watercolour paints. Colours are then taken up on the brush, which has been dipped in water. When painted onto a surface, the water evaporates but the gum arabic remains, and binds the pigment to the surface.

Heightening The application of areas of gouache (usually white) to highlight features in a watercolour.

Illuminated manuscript A manuscript decorated with small illustrations, or "illuminations".

Ink Ink has often been used with watercolours, to provide an outline to which watercolour is added, or as an integral part of the painting. During the Renaissance, ink was made from diseased parts of oak trees. By the 16th century, artists used carbon ink, a mix of charcoal and gum. In China and India, this was hardened by baking, and a sheen was created by adding resin.

Glaze A thin layer of gum arabic

Lead white Lead carbonate. Once used to make watercolour opaque.

Limner A 17th-century term used to describe someone who painted in opaque watercolours. It comes from the medieval Latin word *illuminare* ("to paint"). Many early miniature painters were known as limners.

Medium The word is used in various different ways: 1) A method used by artists – painting and sculpture are two different media. 2) A material – for example, oil paint or watercolour. 3) The liquid in which pigments are suspended – for example, gum and water is the medium used for watercolour.

Miniature Normally used to describe a small portrait painted in any type of watercolour. The term's origins lie in the Latin word *minium*, which means "red lead". Red lead was used as a base colour by early miniaturists. In doing this, they were adopting the tradition followed by many late medieval manuscript illuminators – "miniature" can also be used to refer to a manuscript illumination.

Palette Modern watercolours are usually mixed in the cavities provided in a box of watercolour paints. Prior to this, separate palettes were used, made from objects such as mussel shells, and later from ivory.

A good brush should come to a fine point

In the later 18th century, watercolours were often mixed on ivory palettes.

Paper
Paper replaced parchment as the painting surface for watercolours. The paper used is usually white, and acts as a reflector of light through transparent washes of colour. Paper is coated with glue or starch, so that ink or watercolours are not soaked up like ink on blotting paper. The first papers were hand-made from the fibres of boiled rags and linen. By the late 18th century, tougher hand-made papers appeared. The 19th century saw the invention of cheaper machine-made paper.

Parchment The skin – usually from sheep, goats, or calves – used in the Middle Ages as a writing and painting surface, particularly for illuminated manuscripts.

Pigment Derived from animal, mineral, or vegetable sources,

Ground pigment pours out of a spout at the front

A "paint mill" (Winsor and Newton, about 1850), used for the grinding of pigments.

pigment gives paint its colour. Ground into small particles, it is held in suspension in a binding agent such as oil (in oil paint) or gum arabic (in watercolours). When paint is struck by light, it is the pigment that gives off the particular colour.

Scraping-out The creation of highlights by scraping away paint to reveal the white paper below.

Stopping-out A technique used to lighten an area of dark colour. While the paint is still wet, colour is lifted off – with a moist cloth, a sponge, or a piece of bread.

Tempera The term is often used to refer to paint in which pigment is mixed (tempered) with egg yolk and thinned with water. It is also applied to pigments dissolved in water and mixed with gum or glue. Today, "tempera" may be used loosely for any watery kind of paint.

Tubes Around 1847, Winsor and Newton developed the first tubes of watercolour. The paint was kept moist by adding honey or glycerine.

Underdrawing Watercolours are often sketched out first in pen or, more usually, pencil.

Vellum A fine parchment, made of young animal skins rubbed with pumice, chalk, or ground bone.

Wash An application of semi-transparent ink or watercolour, as opposed to the use of gouache or opaque bodycolour.

Watercolour The general term used to describe paints soluble in water.

Wet-on-wet Working on paper that has been deliberately dampened with water (or where the paint is still wet) so that colours run into each other.

Woodcut A relief print made from cutting out a design drawn onto the surface of a wooden block. When the inked block is printed onto paper, it is the cut-out areas that remain white.

Featured works

Look here to find the location of, and complete details about, the works featured in the book.

This section also includes photographic acknowledgments. Every effort has been made to trace the copyright holders, and we apologise in advance for any unintentional omissions. We would

THE CRUCIFIXION, French Psalter, c.1215 (p. 11)

be pleased to insert the appropriate acknowledgment in any subsequent edition of this publication.
t: top; b: bottom; c: centre; l: left; r: right

Abbreviations:
AIC: © The Art Institute of Chicago, All Rights Reserved; BAL: Bridgeman Art Library, London; BL: By permission of the British Library, London; BM: The Trustees of the British Museum, London; CM: Castle Museum, Norwich; ML: Musée du Louvre, Paris; NPG: By courtesy of the National Portrait Gallery, London; OAG: Oldham Art Gallery, Oldham, Lancashire; RIBA: The British Architectural Library, RIBA, London; RMN: Réunion des Musées Nationaux, Paris; TG: Tate Gallery, London; V&A: Courtesy of the Board of Trustees of the V&A, London; WMG: William Morris Gallery, Walthamstow, London; W&N: Winsor and Newton, Harrow, Middlesex

Front cover: Clockwise from top left: Ivory palettes, W&N; Egyptian tools (p7); *Standing Female Nude* (p55); *The Heneage Jewel* (p24); watercolour box, W&N; *The Military Roll of Arms* (p8); lady's silver paint pot, (p40); *Rosa Damascena* (p9); St. John's Gospel (p10). **Inside front flap:** *t: Young Man Among Roses* (p25); *b:* Egyptian upright slab (p7); **Back cover:** Clockwise from top left: Locket paint set and catalogue (p29); *Peasant Girl with Turkeys* (p50); *Gallery of the Society of Painters in Watercolours* (p38); cake-maker (p7); *The Roman Campagna* (detail), and *c* (p7); *A Falcon* (p21); *Three Studies of a Helmet* (p16); portable paint set (p29); artist's taborette (p23); pigment grinder, W&N; October (p13); *Sunflowers* (p59)

p1: (Half Title): Watercolour box, W&N. **p2:** *tl: The Ancient Pine of Dong Mon* (p19); *tr:* Detail from page of Moralized Bible (p11); *cr: Study of a Velvet Crab* (p14); *cr:* Design for a Single Flower of Tulip Chintz (p48); *b: The Bodhisattva Manjusri* (p20-1); *cl:* Garden of Eden (p13); *tc:* Gold leaf, W&N. **p3: (Title Page):** *tl:* William Blake, title pages to Young's *"Night Thoughts"* (p42); *tc: St.*

Germain Near Tunis (p58); *tr: Sir Walter Raleigh* (p24); *b: Peasant Girl with Turkeys* (p50-51). **p4:** *tc: A Monk Resisting the Attractions of Women* (p20); *cr: The Heneage Jewel* (p24); *br: Nightmare of Demons and Chimeras* (p18); *bc:* Plan of Half of the Mosaic Cupola of Santa Costanza, Rome, (p8-9); *tl:* Watercolour box, W&N; *bl:* Gum arabic, W&N; *tr:* Cinnabar and saffron, W&N **p5:** *The Three Bathers* (p52)

Pages 6-7 What is watercolour?
p6: *tl:* Hand and ritual markings, The Ancient Art and Architecture Collection; *cr:* Egyptian upright slab, BM; *bl:* Egyptian brushes, palettes, and pigments, BM. **p7:** *tl: The Ancient Pine of Dong Mon*, Gao Fengham (see p19); *bl:* View of the Campagna, Italy, J.M.W. Turner, TG; *br:* watercolour cake-maker, watercolour cakes and tubes, W&N; *c:* gum arabic, W&N; *tr:* Shah Tahmasb's *Nizami Manuscript*, BL

Pages 8-9 The variety of watercolour
p8: *tl:* Map of Great Britain, Matthew Paris, BL; *cr: The Military Roll of Arms*, BL; *cl: St. Ottilie*, Staatliche Graphische Sammlung, Munich; *bc:* Plan of Half of the Cupola of Santa Costanza, Rome, Pietro Santi Bartoli, RIBA. **p9:** Wimpole Hall: Front Entrance from Repton's Red Book (before & after planting proposed), Humphry Repton, © National Trust 1991, AC Cooper; *cl: Calais Pier*, David Cox, Spink and Son Ltd., London/BAL; *cr: Rosa Damascena* from *Les Roses*, Pierre-Joseph Redouté, Lindley Library RHS/BAL; *br:* Dulwich Picture Gallery, Sir John Soane, Sir John Soane's Museum, London

Pages 10-11 Illuminated texts
p10: *cl:* Beginning of St. John's Gospel, *Arnstein Bible*, BL; *br:* St. John, *Lindisfarne Gospels*, BL; *tr:* Jacob Wrestling with the Angel, *Vienna Genesis*, National Library, Vienna. **p11:** *tl: The Crucifixion*, French Psalter, Musée Marmottan, Paris; *bl: Siege Warfare*, BL; *br: Baptism of Constantine* Initial, Girolamo di Giovanni da Cremona, Musée Marmottan, Paris; *cr:* A King, a Queen and a Cleric Instructing a Secular Artist in the Writing, and Painting of a Manuscript, Moralized Bible, Pierpont Morgan Library, New York; *tr:* Mussel shell

Pages 12-13 The Limbourgs
p12: *Les Très Riches Heures du Duc de Berry*; *bl:* January; *tr:* Calendar for January; *bc:* February; *br:* March. **p13:** *tl:* October; *b:* The Garden of Eden, Musée Condé, Chantilly/Giraudon, Paris; *tr:* Gold leaf, W&N

Pages 14-15 Nature into art
p14: *tl:* Bramble, *Herbarium*, Apuleius Platonicus, Bodleian Library, Oxford; *bl: A White-Headed Parrot, Tortoise-Shell and Rock Underwing Butterflies an Oak Beauty Moth and White Muscadine Grapes*, Samuel Dixon, The National Gallery of Ireland; *cr: Daffodils and Red Admiral Butterfly*, Jacques le Moyne de Morgues, V&A. **p15:** *tc: Study of a Velvet Crab*, John Ruskin, Ashmolean Museum, Oxford; *bl: Jumping Trout*, Winslow Homer, The Brooklyn Museum New York, 41.220, In Memory of Dick S. Ramsa; *br:* W. Homer's paint box, W&N

Pages 16-17 Watercolour's first master
p16: *tr: Self Portrait*, Albrecht Dürer, Alte Pinakothek, Munich; *c: Three Studies of a Helmet*, Dürer, ML, RMN; *cl: A Weierhaus*, Dürer, BM; *cr: Stag Beetle*, Dürer, Collection of the J. Paul Getty Museum, Malibu, California; *bl: Dream Vision*, Dürer, Kunsthistorisches Museum, Vienna. **p17** *View of the Val d'Arco, Tyrol*, Dürer, ML, RMN

Pages 18-19 Eastern approaches
p18: *c: Animals and Their Uses*, BL; *bl:* Shah Tahmasb's *Nizami Manuscript*, BL; *r: Nightmare of Demons and Chimeras*, Kawanabe Nobuyuki ("Kyosai"), BM. **p19:** *t: The Ancient Pine of Dong Mon*, Gao Fengham, BM; *br:* Portrait of Cai Shiying, BM; *cl: Two Popular Ethiopian Saints*, BL; *bl: The Adventures of Prince Panji*, BL

Pages 20-21 The art of India
p20: *t: The Bodhisattva Manjusri*, BL; *c: A Monk*

Resisting the Attractions of Women, V&A; *bl: Akbar's Triumphant Entry into Surat*, V&A; *cr: The Awakening of Kumbhakarna*, Sahib Din, BL. **p21:** *tr: The Toils of Love*, BL; *cr: A Falcon or Peregrine*, BL; *cl: The Book of Creation*, BL

Pages 22-23 Miniature painting
p22: *tr: Mrs Pemberton*, Hans Holbein, V&A; *cr:* Hans Holbein, Lucas Hornebolte, Wallace Collection; *bl: The Family of Sir Thomas More*, Rowland Lockey, V&A. **p23:** *tl: Baroness Burdett-Coutts*, William Charles Ross, NPG; *cr: Sir Thomas Stepney*, George Engleheart, V&A; *bl: William Grimaldi at His Writing Desk*, Mary Grimaldi, Louisa Edwards, NPG; *br:* Artist's taborette for painting miniatures, W&N

Pages 24-25 Portrait of an era
p24: *tr: Self Portrait*, Nicholas Hilliard, V&A; *cr: The Heneage ("Armada") Jewel*, Hilliard, V&A; *bl: George Clifford*, Hilliard, National Maritime Museum Library, London; *tr: Sir Walter Raleigh*, Hilliard, NPG **p25:** *Young Man Among Roses*, Hilliard, V&A; *tr:* Mussel shell, W&N

Pages 26-27 Exploring new worlds
p26: *tr:* World map; *br: Eskimo Woman and Child*, John White, BM; *cl:* Livingstone's compass, Royal Geographical Society, London; *bl: The Village of Pomeiooc*, John White, BM. **p27:** *t: A Prospect of the Land and Forts... Before Tangier*, Wenzel Hollar, BM; *cl: Chinese Barges of Lord Macartney's Embassy Preparing to Pass under a Bridge*, William Alexander, BM; *cr: Colonnes du Temple de Zeus Olympien, Athène*, Dominique Papety, ML/RMN; *bl: The Theatre at Miletus*, William Pars, BM; *bc:* Hooker's Pouch, Royal Geographical Society, London

Pages 28-29 The portable art
p28: *cl:* Watercolour box, W&N *tr: An Artist Travelling in Wales*, Thomas Rowlandson, BM; *cr: Messieurs les Voyageurs in a Snow Drift upon Mount Tarrar*, J.M.W. Turner, BM; *bc: Ruins of Paestum near Salerno: The Three Temples*, John Robert Cozens, OAG. **p29:** *t: Tivoli From Below the Waterfalls*, Francis Towne, BM; *cl:* Eugène Delacroix, Page from *Album du Maroc*, ML/RMN; *c:* Portable paint set, W&N; *br:* W&N catalogue and locket paint set, W&N

Pages 30-31 Satirical images
p30: *cl: Sketching a Country Woman*, Thomas Rowlandson, Museum of New Zealand, Te Papa Tongarewa, Wellington, NZ; *tr: George III and Napoleon*, James Gillray, Mary Evans Picture Library; *bc: John Bull and his Family Taking Leave of the Income Tax*, Roberts, Neil McCann. **p31:** *tr: Two Drinkers*, Honoré Daumier, Christie's Colour Library; *tl: Le Désaccord*, Alexandre Gabriel Decamps, ML/RMN; *c: Caricature Portrait of the Political Journalist Henri Rochefort*, Alfred Le Petit, Bacholet, Paris; *br: Maggie Thatcher*, David Lewis; *bl: Sir Cecil Harcourt Smith Receives a Deputation from a Northern Town That is Meditating a Museum*, Sir Max Beerbohm, V&A

Pages 32-33 The British tradition
p32: *tl:* John Constable, Daniel Maclise, NPG; *c: Folkestone Harbour with a Rainbow*, John Constable, BM. **p33:** *tl: Monument to Perpetuate the Fame of British Artists*, James Prinsep, BM; *tr: Kirkstall Abbey, Yorkshire*, Thomas Girtin, V&A; *bl: The Night Train*, David Cox, Birmingham Museum and Art Gallery; *cr: Landscape*, John Martin, OAG

Pages 34-35 Cotman – a sense of place
p34: *tl:* Portrait of John Sell Cotman after J.P. Davis, Mrs Dawson Turner, CM; *bl: Devil's Elbow, Rokeby Park*, Cotman, CM; *br: Greta Bridge*, Cotman, CM. **p35:** *br: Storm on Yarmouth Beach*, Cotman, CM; *tc: Greta Bridge*, Cotman, BM; *bl:* Yarmouth Beach During a Storm from *In and About Ancient Yarmouth*, Norfolk County Council Library and Information Service/Photo: Brian Ollington

Pages 36-37 Turner and landscape
p36: *tl:* Turner's House, Cheyne Walk, NPG/Photo: Emery Walker; *cl:* Turner Painting

One of his Pictures, Richard Doyle, NPG; *tr: J.M.W. Turner*, C. Martin, NPG; *cl: Imaginary Landscape with Windsor Castle*, Turner, TG. **p37:** *tl: The Sun Setting Amongst Clouds*, Turner, TG; *tr:* Turner, TG; *br: The Old Devil's Bridge, Pass of St. Gothard*, Turner, TG; *c: View of the Campagna* (p7); *tr:* Turner's palette and travelling case, TG

Pages 38-39 Exhibition works
p38: *tl:* Exhibition medals, W&N; *bl: A Village Snow Scene*, Robert Hills, Yale Center for British Art, Paul Mellon Collection; *tr: Gallery of the Society of Painters in Watercolours*, Thomas Rowlandson, BM; *br: L'Escalier du Musée*, Jean-Baptiste Isabey, ML/RMN/Giraudon. **p39:** *tl: Stonehenge*, John Constable, V&A; *cl: The Thames at Isleworth*, John Glover, Yale Center for British Art; *bc: A Frank Encampment in the Desert of Mt. Sinai 1842*, John Frederick Lewis, Yale Center for British Art, Paul Mellon Collection; *cl:* W&N watercolour box, W&N

STONEHENGE, John Constable, 1836 (p. 39)

Pages 40-41 A genteel pursuit
p40: *tr: Man With a Claude Glass*, Thomas Gainsborough, BM; *tl:* Archibald Robertson's Trade Card, BM; *cl:* Lady's silver paint pot; *bc: Two Young Women Drawing Amidst Classical Ruins*, Hubert Robert, ML/RMN. **p41:** *tl: Scene in Wales*, Rev. Thomas Gisborne, BM; *cr: Sketching Party in Leigh Woods*, Samuel Jackson, Bristol Museum and Art Gallery; *tr:* Camera obscura, Science Museum, London

Pages 42-43 The "mystics"
p42: *tl:* Drawing of William Blake, Hulton Deutsch Collection; *cl: (left)* Illustration to Young's *"Night Thoughts"*, Night III, title page, *(right)* illustration to Young's *"Night Thoughts"*, Night VIII, Narcissa, William Blake, BM/BAL; *tr: Mildew Blighting Ears of Corn*, William Blake, National Trust, Petworth/BAL; *br: Jacob's Dream*, William Blake, BM; *bl: The Herdsman*, Samuel Palmer, OAG. **p43:** *tl: Port Stragglin*, Richard Dadd, BM; *tr: Phaeton*, Gustave Moreau, ML/RMN; *bl: The Primitive City*, Edward Calvert, BM

Pages 44-45 Book illustrations
p44: *cl: Cinderella*, BL; *bl:* Illustration from *Oliver Twist*, George Cruikshank, BM; *br:* Heathcliff from *Wuthering Heights*, Edmund Dulac, Sotheby's; *tr: Girl and Two Babies*, Kate Greenaway, V&A. **p45:** *cl: Thumbelina*, Joan Charleton, Sotheby's; *cr: Treasure Island*, Salomon von Abbé, Sotheby's; *tl:* Winnie the Pooh, Line Illustration from WINNIE-THE-POOH, copyright E.H. Shepard under the Berne Convention. In the U.S.

Continued on p. 64

THE AWAKENING OF KUMBHAKARNA, Sahib Din, 1652 (p. 20)

ODALISQUE, J.D. Ingres, 1864 (p. 54)

Index

Continued from p. 63

copyright 1926 by E.P. Dutton, copyright renewal 1954 by A.A.Milne. Colouring-in copyright © 1973 by E.H.Shepard and Methuen Children's Books Ltd. Reproduced by permission of Curtis Brown Ltd, London; *br*: Pop-up Rupert Bear, Photo: R.Kemp, by kind permission of Express Newspapers plc

Pages 46-47 The Pre-Raphaelites
p46: *cl*: *The Mill on the Thames at Mapledurham,* George Price Boyce, Fitzwilliam Museum, Cambridge; *tr*: *Horatio Discovering the Madness of Ophelia,* Dante Gabriel Rossetti, OAG; *b*: *Chaffinch Nest and May Blossom,* William Henry Hunt, Courtauld Institute Galleries, London; *tc*: Lewis Carroll, Rossetti Family, NPG. **p47:** *tl*: *Phyllis and Demophoön,* Sir Edward Coley Burne-Jones, Birmingham Museum and Art Gallery; *tr*: Sir Edward Coley Burne-Jones, photo: Barbara Leighton, NPG; *cr*: *The Painter's Pleasure,* Simeon Solomon, Whitworth Gallery, University of Manchester; *br*: *The Holy City,* William Holman Hunt, OAG

Pages 48-49 A company of craftsmen
p48: *tr*: *Portrait of William Morris,* Cosmo Rowe, National Trust Photographic Library/Derrick E. Witty, Wightwick Manor; *cl*: *Trellis Wallpaper Design,* WMG; *bl*: Piece of Tulip Chintz and Printing Block, WMG; *br*: Design for Single Flower of Tulip Chintz, WMG. **p49:** Design for Pomona Tapestry, National Trust Photographic Library/Derrick E.Witty, Wightwick Manor, West Midlands

Pages 50-51 Impressionism
p50: *bc*: *Peasant Girl with Turkeys,* Camille Pissarro, Brooklyn Museum, 59.28, gift of Mrs. Edwin C.Vogel/Brooklyn Museum Collection; *tr*: *Portrait of Berthe Morisot,* Edouard Manet, Helen Regenstein Collection, 1963.812, AIC; *bl*: *Carriage in the Bois de Boulogne,* Berthe Morisot,

Ashmolean Museum, Oxford. **p51:** *t*: *Landscape Near La Côte Saint André,*J.B. Jongkind, BM; *c*: *Gondoliers at Venice,* J.L.E. Meissonier, ML/RMN; *br*: *Tahitian Landscape,* Paul Gauguin, ML/RMN; *tl*: *Study of Woman of Algiers,* Eugène Delacroix, ML/RMN

Pages 52-53 Cézanne – art and light
p52: *tl*: Photograph of Cézanne, Hulton Deutsch Collection; *tr*: *Man Wearing a Straw Hat,* Paul Cézanne, gift of Janis Palmer in memory of Pauline K.Palmer 1983.1498, AIC; *bl*: *The Three Bathers,* Cézanne, National Museum of Wales, Cardiff; *br*: *Mont Ste. Victoire,* Cézanne, Courtauld Institute Galleries, London. **p53:** *Still Life with Apples, Bottles, and Chairback,* Cézanne, Courtauld Institute Galleries, London

Pages 54-55 The nude in watercolour
p54: *cl*: *Painting Under Difficulties,*Thomas Rowlandson, National Gallery of Scotland; *tr*: *Odalisque,* J.D. Ingres, Musée Bonnat, Bayonne; *b*: *Les Deux Amies,* Jules-Robert Auguste, ML, Cabinet des Dessins/RMN; *tl*: *Standing Female Nude,* Paul Cézanne, ML, Cabinet des Dessins/RMN. **p55:** *tr*: *Reclining Female Nude,* Oskar Kokoschka, Graphische Sammlung, Albertina, Vienna © DACS 1993; *br*: *Neptune,* Auguste Rodin, Paris, photo: Bruno Jarret, © ADAGP, Paris and DACS, London 1993; *bl*: Auguste Rodin, photo: G.C. Beresford, NPG

Pages 56-57 Modern uses of the medium
p56: *cl*: Design for a Nursery Chintz, Charles Voysey, RIBA; *bc*: Stage Design for *Comte Ory,* Glyndebourne, Oliver Messel,V&A Theatre Museum, reproduced by kind permission of Lord Snowdon. **p57:** *tl*: Design for Corniche Mosque, Abdel Wahed El-Wakil, El-Wakil Associates; *tr*: *Kent, Garden of Eden,* Frank Sherwin, reproduced by kind permission of the keeper of the National Railway Museum, York; *cr*: Cloak from Hansel and Gretel, Roger A.

Oakes, costume design by Terry Frances Parr, reproduction courtesy of Welsh National Opera, photo: Kurt Vickery; *br*: Fashion design, Emma Mandell-Lynn

Pages 58-59 Expressionism
p58: *cl*: *Russian Prisoner of War,* Egon Schiele, gift of Dr. Eugene Solow in memory of Gloria Blackstone Solow, 1966.172 recto, photograph by Kathleen Culbert-Aguilar, Chicago, © 1992 AIC; *bl*: *Das Paar,* George Grosz, Christie's Colour Library © DACS 1993; *cr*: *St. Germain Near Tunis,* August Macke, Städtische Galerie im Lenbachhaus, Munich; *tr*: *Two Blue Horses in Front of a Red Rock,* Franz Marc, Städtische Galerie im Lenbachhaus, Munich. **p59:** *Sunflowers,* Emil Nolde, Visual Arts Library, © Nolde – Stiftung, Seebüll

Pages 60-61 Into the abstract world
p60: *cl*: *Head of a Woman,* Pablo Picasso, gift of Mr. and Mrs. Roy J. Friedman, 1964.215, photograph by Kathleen Culbert-Aguilar, Chicago, photograph courtesy of AIC, © DACS 1993; *bl*: Photograph of Picasso, Hulton Deutsch Collection; *cr*: *La Fleur Polychrome,* Fernand Léger, Musée des Beaux Arts, Lyon © DACS 1993; *tr*: *Hinein,* Wassily Kandinsky, Sprengel Museum, Hannover, © ADAGP, Paris and DACS, London 1993. **p61:** *t*: *Stilleben mit dem Apfel,* Paul Klee, Christie's Colour Library, © DACS 1993; *bl*: *Northwest Drift,* Mark Tobey, TG © DACS 1993; *br*: *Untitled,* Anish Kapoor, TG

Pages 62-63 Glossary
p62: *tl*: Moralized Bible (see p11); *bl*: Watercolour Box, W&N *tr*: Pigment Grinder, *c*: Ivory Palettes, W&N. **p63:** *tl*: The Crucifixion, French Psalter (see p11); *br*: Odalisque, J.D.Ingres (see p54); *cr*: Stonehenge, John Constable (see p39); *bl*: The Awakening of Kumbhakarna, Sahib Din, (see p20)

Acknowledgments

Dorling Kindersley would like to thank: Winsor & Newton for allowing us to photograph at its museum in Harrow, Middlesex; and the staff at Winsor & Newton who answered our innumerable questions; the William Morris Gallery, Walthamstow, London, which allowed us to photograph their collection; Alan Brett Ltd, for giving us permission to photograph their maps; Greg Martin, for taking an interest in the book and providing us with information about his map; Neil McCann, for kindly lending us his Roberts' print; Hilary Bird, for preparing the index.

Thanks are also due to the following members of the Eyewitness Art Team: Margaret Chang, Sandra Copp, Gwen Edmonds, Sean Moore, Toni Rann, Job Rabkin, and Tina Vaughan; a special thank you goes to: Louise Candlish, Mark Johnson-Davies, Phil Hunt, Laura Harper, Stephanie Jackson, and Constance Novis for their help and exceptional kindness.

A special thank you is also due to Julia Harris-Voss, for her work on additional picture research, and for her unerring support throughout the project.

Author's acknowledgments:
I would like to thank the following people for their invaluable help on this book: Helen Castle, Laura Harper, Ann Kay, and Claire Pegrum; and I would like to dedicate this book to my children: Alexander, Oliver, and Emily.